FLOWER
INNOVATIONS

PAULA PRYKE

Photography by **KEVIN SUMMERS**

MITCHELL BEAZLEY

for **PETER**

FLOWER INNOVATIONS
PAULA PRYKE

Photographs by **KEVIN SUMMERS**

First published in Great Britain by Mitchell Beazley,
an imprint of Reed Consumer Books Limited,
Michelin House, 81 Fulham Road, London SW3 6RB
and Auckland, Melbourne, Singapore and Toronto

Art Director **JACQUI SMALL**
Art Editor **TRINITY FRY**

Executive Editor **JUDITH MORE**
Senior Editor **JANE STRUTHERS**
Production **MICHELLE THOMAS**

© Reed International Books Ltd 1995
Text copyright © Paula Pryke 1995

A CIP record for this book is available from the British Library.

ISBN 1-85732-568-0

The publishers have made every effort to ensure that all instructions
given in this book are accurate and safe, but they cannot accept
liability for any resulting injury, damage or loss to either person or
property whether direct or consequential and howsoever arising.
The author and publishers will be grateful for any information
which will assist them in keeping future editions up to date.

Colour reproduction by Mandarin Offset Singapore
Printed and bound in China

FLOWER
INNOVATIONS

CONTENTS

Half-title page: A sunflower (*Helianthus annus* 'Teddy Bear').

Title page: 'Confetti', 'Nicole' and 'Tamango' spray roses (*Rosa*),

bound with a skirt of banana (*Musa*) leaves.

Previous page: 'Nappi' heliconias (*Heliconia*) with dried honeysuckle

(*Lonicera*) vine twisted around the heliconia stems. Because of their watery

origins, I was inspired to use one of the heliconia flowers upside down

in this submerged arrangement. Erect heliconias are perfect for

this as they have bracts which rise above the flowers and act

as supports when the blooms are inverted.

Right: Fruit and vegetables add texture and take the place of foliage in

this colourful arrangement of arum lilies (*Zantedeschia*), *Leucospermum*,

Leucadendron 'Safari Sunset', germini (*Gerbera*) and 'Red Velvet'

roses (*Rosa*). The flowers are arranged in groups of three.

INTRODUCTION

Throughout history, flowers have stimulated us and enhanced and improved our lives. They grace all our important festivals and ceremonies, and are a token of comfort and compassion on sad occasions. They often figure prominently in the emotional moments in our lives. "We cannot fathom the mystery of a single flower, nor is it intended that we should." The words of the English nineteenth-century art critic, John Ruskin, perfectly sum up how I feel about the wonders of nature. I am fascinated by the individual personality of each flower, and in the arrangements in this book I have tried to make the flowers speak for themselves.

Man's influence on nature, and the tremendous advances that have been made in horticulture, have brought us bigger and better hybrids with longer flowering seasons, so now we can appreciate the once-rare *Cymbidium* orchid as a common flower and have tulips in our homes every week of the year.

In addition, the enormous improvements in refrigerated transportation, and air travel in particular, have led to flowers which are grown all around the world being sold in many different countries. Sixty percent of the flowers sold worldwide are grown in the Netherlands, where millions of blooms are also traded each year at the Dutch flower auctions. Flowers sold at these auctions come from such diverse locations as Thailand, the West Indies, Kenya, Zimbabwe, Israel, Colombia, Greece, Italy, France, Australia and New Zealand.

Right: A rose tree consisting of 'Nicole', 'Confetti' and 'Yellow Success' roses (*Rosa*), with a trunk made from birch (*Betula*) twigs set in a base of cement. 'Arabian Night' dahlias (*Dahlia*) have been arranged in floral foam placed on top of the cement.

Overleaf, left: 'Negrita' tulips (*Tulipa*) mixed with anemones (*Anemone*) and 'Mainzer Fastnach' roses (*Rosa*), encircled with cabbage leaves.

Overleaf, right: 'Rococo' parrot tulips (*Tulipa*), ivy (*Hedera*) berries, anemones (*Anemone*) and 'Vicky Brown' roses (*Rosa*) make this posy look very warm and festive.

The freshest flowers come from your own garden and from local markets which sell locally grown flowers. Commercially available flowers, which may have travelled halfway around the world, are far from fresh when they first arrive at your local florist. Before the flowers reach the shop they will have been harvested, post-harvest treated if necessary, sent to a local market and then sold by a wholesaler to your retailer. On average, when cut flowers arrive at a florist's shop, they will already be at least three days old, and more often four or five. This is why conditioning the flowers is so important, because you must replace their lost energy supplies and water. To do this, trim at least 1 inch (2.5 cm) off the flowers' stems at an angle with a pair of sharp scissors or secateurs, then place them in a clean container to which you have added fresh, tepid water and flower-food. The best way to clean a container is to wash it thoroughly, using a bottle brush if necessary, in warm water to which you have added a few drops of household bleach. (You may wish to wear rubber gloves while doing this.) This procedure kills bacteria which would otherwise shorten the life of the cut flowers. Let the flowers have a good drink for a couple of hours, then arrange them in a clean container with more fresh water and flower-food. Another factor that is crucial to the longevity of your arrangement is room temperature. Generally speaking, the warmer the room, the faster the flowers will fade – most flowers last longer in cool temperatures of about 50° F (10° C) than they do at about 68° F (20° C) or more.

An easy way to make sure that you buy good-quality flowers is to use the same florist regularly, because he or she will get to know you and will give you the most honest advice, especially at times when good-quality cut flowers are in short supply, such as during Christmas or near Valentine's Day in the northern hemisphere. Even the highest-quality florists may sell disappointing flowers at these times. Most of the materials mentioned in this book should be available from your local florist, which is another reason for having a regular supplier. (As an alternative, some garden centres sell packs of florist's sundries, and flower arranging clubs have sales tables and mail order catalogues for enthusiasts.) Asking for sundries in a florist's shop when you have not bought any flowers can produce a frosty response, so when purchasing

the flowers it is best to explain what you plan to make and to ask whether you will need any special equip-

ment. Floral foam, which is a key ingredient for supporting arrangements, is sold in a vast range of sizes

and shapes, so you may have to be very specific when ordering a special item. You need green floral foam

for fresh flowers, and brown foam for dried flowers. Most shapes can be carved with a sharp knife out of

small rectangular blocks, and very large blocks are also available. Before use, float the green foam on the

surface of a solution of water and flower-food until it sinks and air bubbles stop rising to the surface; do

not over-soak the foam or it may disintegrate, and use it only once. Where possible, you should use wire

mesh in preference to floral foam because the flowers will last much longer. As well as foam, you may

need florist's wires to shape arrangements; these are sold in a variety of gauges. Floral scissors, secateurs

and knives are essential, and their blades must be kept sharp. You may also need other materials, such as

string, rope and raffia; ribbons; double-sided adhesive tape; floral foam tape; floral foam fix; florist's

"frogs"; pin holders; and candle-cups for decorating candlesticks. Finally, you need a good collection of

containers, which must always be kept scrupulously clean. Whenever possible, think up new ideas for

containers, and experiment with covering them in natural products such as coir or sisal matting, or even

sacking. For extravagant parties you can swathe containers in tulle or silk, tied with

ribbon or cord. Old cans and jars also make interesting containers for

flowers and, if necessary, can be camouflaged with fabric, leaves,

stems and even sheets of newspaper. The more inventive you

are, the more original and striking your designs will be.

There is no need for you to reproduce slavishly the

designs in this book – they are simply a guideline from

which you can make your own innovations. Designing

with flowers is an exhilarating experience, so do not feel

constrained by all my suggestions. I am often told that I

break all the rules, but there should not be any rules for

artistic self-expression. To design well with nature you must use

your own senses and your awareness of balance, colour and style.

Archaeologists are said to have found roses in fossilized remains that are over 30 million years old. The Ancient Romans used roses in practically every aspect of their lives – they were a symbol for intrigue, celebration and medicine. It is claimed that Cleopatra wooed Mark Antony with rose oil and rose petals, and certainly today's lovers know all about the seductive power of roses.

Despite their worldwide cultivation, roses are still considered to be a luxury. My favourite story of Ancient Rome concerns the Emperor Nero who held the most lavish parties, with roses and the scent of rose oil everywhere. At one party, guests suffocated under a deluge of rose petals that were released into the air. Nero's tremendous extravagance with roses was said to be one of the reasons for the collapse of the Roman Empire. Rose-lovers, you have been warned...

The rose's natural habitat is the northern hemisphere; rose seeds need a cool period in order to germinate. Since early times, roses have been important flowers for collectors and in the sixteenth century they were imported from China via the Silk Route to stock the Mogul emperors' gardens in India. It is these Bengal roses which are among the most important cultivars for the modern hybrids we know so well. Many trading companies imported roses and the East India Company shipped plants to Europe along the spice routes.

Above: A simple arrangement of a dozen red roses has been given an unusual twist with gnarled branches and one fish-tail palm leaf.

The rose has been significant in many cultures. The rose, the myrtle (*Myrtus*) and the apple (*Malus*) were all sacred to the goddess of love, known as Aphrodite to the Greeks and as Venus to the Romans. When she pricked herself on some rose thorns, red roses were said to have sprung from the ground where her blood fell. During the medieval period the rose was used during Mass and rosary beads – a prayer wheel to allow detachment of the mind – were originally constructed from the fragrant paste of crushed rose petals. The British royal family have used the rose as a heraldic symbol and, in 1986, it was adopted by the Americans as a floral emblem.

If you intend to pick roses from your garden, it is best to cut them either in the morning or the evening when the sun is low. Cut the flowers at an angle and immediately place them in water – it is best to carry a bucket of water with you. Do not delay in doing this otherwise an air-lock will form in the stems which will prevent the flowers taking up water. Once back in the house, fill up the bucket until the roses are up to their necks in water, then add flower-food and let them have a good drink. Rose hips also make very useful additions to arrangements and are produced by the rose at the end of the season if you have not dead-headed it. Hips, too, should be placed in water quickly, otherwise the leaves may shrivel up and die.

ROSES

Left: A scented Ecuadorian deep pink rose called 'Preference'.

Above, from left to right: This golden rose with red edging is 'Ambience' and opens beautifully, like a traditional garden rose;

this pink-edged cream rose is 'La Minuet'; the climbing garden rose 'Danse de Feu'; the large-headed golden rose, 'Yellow

Success', is very long-lasting; my favourite two-toned burgundy 'Nicole' rose is available throughout the year.

Since earliest times, the rose (*Rosa*) has been one of the most cherished and commonly cultivated flowers. It

has a special place in most people's hearts and is the world's favourite flower, with billions sold each year.

Roses are extremely versatile for florists and grow in so many varieties and forms that they can be used in

almost every conceivable area of floristry. They are as happy in a vase of water as they are in floral foam,

in which they last a long time and perform well. The tiny micro roses known as 'Serena', and largely culti-

vated in Italy, have heads less than ½ inch (1 cm) across. They make sweet flowerheads for circlets or tied

posies for place settings at a very special function. At the other end of the scale, the 3-feet (1-metre) long,

large-headed and long-lasting roses are perfect for grand displays.

Above: Roses can be used to base an arrangement (*see pages 16–17*) and are best when fully open, as they provide better cover.

Groups of five of each colour are distributed throughout this arrangement, with an edging of heart-shaped *Galax* leaves.

I used 'Ambience', 'Yellow Success', 'Red Velvet', 'Oceania' and 'Pasadena' roses.

TOPIARY ROSE TREE

MATERIALS

Large bunch of birch (*Betula*) twigs

Heavy florist's wire

Ball of floral foam

Floral foam tape

Sharp knife

'Honesty' roses (*Rosa*)

'Mainzer Fastnach' roses

'Rhapsody' roses

1 Gather together a group of dried birch twigs, then make them into a bundle by wrapping heavy florist's wire around them. Floral foam balls are available from florists, but it is very easy to carve a round shape from a square block if you prefer. Soak the ball in water, then carefully impale it on the top of the twigs. At this stage, you can wrap floral foam tape around the base of the ball if you are uncertain about its stability. Using a sharp knife, trim the twigs at the base so the tree is balanced and stands upright.

2 Cut the rose stems to less than 1 inch (2.5 cm) long, otherwise they will damage the foam ball. Place groups of three roses around the ball at intervals. The rose used here is 'Honesty', which

is an old-fashioned scented variety with green-tinged outer petals.

3 Taking the 'Mainzer Fastnach' roses next, place them in groups of three around the ball, next to the groups of 'Honesty' roses. Try to work out where they will look best before placing them in the floral foam, as too many holes in the ball may cause the foam to disintegrate.

Place the 'Rhapsody' roses in the remaining spaces to create this sugary pink patchwork of scented roses (*right*). This same idea could be used with twigs that have been cemented into a terracotta pot. Alternatively, a ball of roses attached to a rope would make a perfect and pretty pompon for a bridesmaid to hold (*see pages 62–3*).

Roses which are grown commercially are cut and treated with flower-food. They are graded and sold by their length, then are transported either in water or in special containers out of water to make sure that they arrive at their destination in perfect condition. When you get them, cut off at least 1 inch (2.5 cm) of stem at an angle, carefully remove any lower foliage, then condition them in water to which flower-food has been added. Removing the thorns can damage the stems and may make the rose prone to bacterial attack, but it is very important if the flowers are going to be used in a tied bouquet. Use a sharp knife to prise off the thorns carefully without damaging the surface of the stems. Roses will last for up to 18 days in the correct conditions. Never crush the stems as this allows bacteria to enter and destroys the stems' capillary action. Frequent misting improves the life of roses and they should be kept in a cool place if possible.

Commercial roses are often recut underwater to make sure that no air-locks occur in their stems. If you purchase roses and condition and arrange them only to find that their heads are drooping, it is likely that they are suffering from an air-lock. If this is the case, you can free the lock by protecting the flowerheads with paper, recutting the stems underwater and immediately dipping them in boiling water for a few seconds. After this, stand the flowers in lukewarm water to which flower-food has been added.

Commercial roses are divided into four main groups. Large-flowering roses, such as the white 'Tineke', are sold in bud and are perfect for buttonholes and wedding work.

Above: A conical summer centre piece of large-headed 'Yellow Success' roses and small, spray 'Yellow Dot' roses, courgette (*Zucchini*) flowers, petalless sunflowers (*Helianthus*), blue and white scabious (*Scabiosa*), with *Hypericum*, *Alchemilla mollis* and green dill (*Anethum graveolens*) for foliage.

Left: In this Victorian posy the flowers are arranged in concentric circles. The top roses are the beautiful rust-coloured 'Leonardis' and the peach roses are 'Versillea'. *Hebe*, *Skimmia japonica* and Arabian chincherinchees (*Ornithogalum*) are encircled with *Cordata* leaves.

Medium-flowering roses, such as 'Gabriella', are sold as slightly open buds. There are small-flowering cultivars, such as the bright pink 'Disco', and there are also bush or spray roses, of which 'White Princess' is one of the most useful. These spray roses are in short supply during the winter months but growers are working to improve this situation.

The best commercial roses are those which grow in hot, sunny climes. The colour of the flowers can be controlled by shading them with different-coloured nets and it is this tactic which makes sure that the massive demand for red roses is met in the middle of each February. Most people believe that it is the flower shops which raise the price of Valentine's Day flowers, but it is the heavy demand which pushes the price up. In the Netherlands all the flowers are sold at a Dutch auction, where the price starts high and goes down. If there is a huge demand for roses, the flower brokers will bid early and inflate the prices. I often have to pay up to five times more for roses during Valentine's week than I would during the week preceding or succeeding it. Sometimes unscrupulous dealers will buy roses when they are inexpensive, then put them in cold storage, ready to bring them out for Valentine's Day. This may mean that you can purchase what appears to be a bargain, but you might be buying very vintage flowers – and, sadly, roses do not mature like a fine wine.

Left: A flat-backed basket with a handle is useful for tying on the ends of pews. This one is filled with 'La Minuet' and 'Henri Matisse' roses and scented sweet peas (*Lathyrus odoratus*) in matching colours.
Right: Heather plants (*Erica*) were pulled through a basket to create this container. The basket was then filled with 'Nicole', 'Mainzer Fastnach' and 'Nikita' roses, deep blue gentians (*Gentiana*), sea holly (*Eryngium maritimum*), blue scabious (*Scabiosa*), eucalyptus (*Eucalyptus*), pink heather and marjoram (*Origanum*).

Right: A fully open standard carnation, *Dianthus* 'New Arthur Sim'.

Above, from left to right: 'Roma' standard carnation; the fluffy petaled, blush-pink 'Shunit'; variegated carnations, like this pink and white 'Dark Pierrot', are generally called "fancy" in the trade and are known by their bi-colour; the scented old-fashioned pink variety known as 'Rosa Monica'; Sweet William (*Dianthus barbatus* 'Cerise'). It can be very misleading to name carnation varieties because each country of origin has different names for very similar-looking varieties. My advice, when buying carnations, is to describe as precisely as possible the exact colour or bi-colour.

C A R N A T I

Carnations are among the most popular flowers in the world which, oddly enough, means they have often received a less than favourable press. Although their botanical name is *Dianthus*, which literally translated from the Greek means "divine", these flowers are maligned by some people because they are so inexpensive, popular and widely available. I do not usually stock standard carnations in my shop and much prefer their seasonal varieties, such as Sweet Williams (*Dianthus barbatus*), which flower in late April and May, and the lovely old-fashioned pinks with their clove scents. However, I chose to honour these defamed blooms by including them in this book because their popularity has made them unfashionable and I simply cannot abide flower snobbery. They are also among the most long-lasting flowers you can buy.

LILY AND FRUIT CENTRE PIECE

MATERIALS

Straight-sided glass bowl

Selection of attractive fruit

Floral foam plastic-backed ring

Sharp knife or pair of secateurs

Senecio

Green dill (*Anethum graveolens*)

Viburnum berries

Rudbeckia

'Peer Gynt' roses (*Rosa*)

'Leonardis' roses

Dark red astilbe (*Astilbe*)

'Royal Gold' lilies (*Lilium regale*)

1 Fill the straight-sided glass bowl with a selection of mouthwatering fruit. It is good to use some fruit that can be cut open to reveal an interesting internal pattern, such as papaya, kiwi and citrus fruits. Here, I used papaya, black cherries with their stems still attached, red currants and strawberries. Make sure that the fruit is in prime condition (you do not want it to spoil before the flowers fade) and choose colours that will complement the flowers.

2 Floral foam rings can be purchased from florists and some garden centres. They are available in different sizes so order your ring to fit the diameter of the glass bowl. Soak the ring in warm water and flower-food, but do not soak it for too long as the floral foam can disintegrate. Half an hour, or until the air bubbles cease rising to the top

is sufficient. Cut the *Senecio* into small sprigs about 2–3 inches (5–7.5 cm) long and cover the floral foam ring with them. The ring will be viewed from the sides when it is placed on a table, so it is important to cover all the black plastic of the ring.

3 Add the foliage to provide interest and texture. The green dill lightens the overall colour and the viburnum berries give a nice droop to the lower line of the arrangement. Next, add the *Rudbeckia*, which has a deep brown centre and yellow petals.

4 Cut the stems of the roses and astilbe so that they are about 2–3 inches (5–7.5 cm) long, then position them throughout the arrangement.

Cut down the lily stems to about 2–3 inches (5–7.5 cm) long, and arrange them throughout the ring (*right*).

3

4

ONS

23

CARNATIONS IN A SAVOY CABBAGE

MATERIALS

Savoy cabbage

Sharp knife

Sheet of plastic

Floral foam

Several heavy florist's wires

Trailing love-lies-bleeding (*Amaranthus*)

Liguster privet (*Ligustrum*) berries

Grape hyacinths (*Muscari*)

Carnations (*Dianthus* 'Scia' and 'Pierrot')

1 Savoy cabbages are particularly good for flower arranging because their soft centres are easy to remove and their leaves have an interesting colour and texture. Trim the base of a fresh cabbage so it sits flat. Now cut out the middle of the cabbage, leaving an outer rim about 1 inch (2.5 cm) thick all around. Line the cabbage with the plastic, then place a small square of moistened floral foam in the middle. Trim it carefully to sit snugly inside the cabbage.

2 Arrange groups of love-lies-bleeding (*Amaranthus*) and privet (*Ligustrum*) berries in small clumps in the middle of the cabbage. For this arrangement, the only foliage is on the privet because the cabbage leaves provide the remainder. The deep red love-lies-bleeding flowers bring out the colour in the carnations and their plumes give movement to the arrangement.

3 Now add groups of grape hyacinths (*Muscari*). Placing flowers in clumps suits a low and textured approach to flower arranging, so choose your material for the contrasts in texture and shape. Make sure that the colours and shapes of the flowers near the cabbage leaves are in sympathy with them and that no ugly patches of bare floral foam are showing through the flowers.

Add clumps of carnations (*right*). Press the cabbage leaves together to keep the arrangement stable. If necessary, you can pin the outer leaves together, using a florist's wire bent into the shape of a hairpin or bobby pin, to increase the stability. However, take care not to puncture the plastic lining when doing this. As the cabbage is lined, it can be placed directly on a table (unless its surface is delicate), although it also looks great on a silver tray or even a simple, round mirror. If the floral foam is regularly moistened and the cabbage kept in a cool place, the arrangement should last for up to ten days. To make a larger centre piece, you could decorate three cabbages and arrange them on a piece of driftwood or a cleaned, old tree root.

The pure white varieties (Z. *aethiopica*) are the most elegant bare-stemmed flowers and they have a very strong presence. Their clean lines make them excellent flowers for modern interiors, and because of the beauty of their calyces they are particularly suitable for all types of floristry. The red, pink and mauve arum lilies are all classified as Z. *rehmannii*, while the yellow, gold and orange ones are Z. *elliottiana*. They all look striking whether arranged on their own or very simply with bear grass (*Dasylirion*), bells of Ireland (*Moluccella laevis*) and contorted willow (*Salix*). The pale yellow variety is the most common and, therefore, the least expensive arum lily. Varieties such as 'Harvest Moon', which is pale yellow, darken with age. The Z. *rehmannii* varies from carmine-red to deep mauve and adds drama to mixed bouquets. I like to use it with burgundies, such as 'Nicole' roses (*Rosa*), love-lies-bleeding (*Amaranthus*) and *Leucadendron* 'Safari Sunset'. The deeper coloured stocks (*Matthiola*) also complement it, as do the lime green of bells of Ireland, spurge (*Euphorbia*) and even the green snapdragon (*Antirrhinum*).

The leaves of arum lilies are useful for flower arranging because they are a good, bright green. Some varieties have spotted foliage, particularly the coloured ones such as 'Black-eyed Beauty', which has a pale creamy yellow spathe with a black eye. Often the pink arums are tinged with deeper colour and some arums look as if they have been splashed with green paint. The Z. *aethiopica* can be completely green, like the 'Green Goddess' variety, or spotted green and white, like the smaller 'Tinkerbell' flowers.

Arum lilies are available all the year around, because when they are not in season in the southern hemisphere they are flowering in the northern hemisphere. These flowers last very well and need simple, regular conditioning and no extra care. When you first get them, trim 1 inch (2.5 cm) or more off their stems at an angle, then place them in a solution of warm water and flower-food. You may notice that their stems have a tendency to split upward, but this does little damage to the flower and produces some interesting curls in clear glass vases. When the water becomes murky, cut off the curly piece of stem and give the flowers some clean water. If you want to avoid this happening, bind some sticky tape around the bottom of the stem to stop it splitting. This is a good tip for making soft stems firmer and stronger before you insert them in floral foam. You can also do this with other hollow-stemmed flowers, such as amaryllis (*Amaryllis*) and delphiniums (*Delphinium*). However, this procedure should not normally be necessary.

Above: A mixture of arum lilies (*Zantedeschia elliottiana* and Z. *rehmannii*) spiralled into a simple tied bunch.

Right: Arum lilies look best arranged very simply. Here they are shown with screw pine (*Pandanus*) and *Ligularia tussilaginea* leaves.

Carnations have three special qualities: the length of their flowering season; the wonderfully fluffy texture of their flowerheads; and their enormous diversity of colour. The *Dianthus* family falls into four categories: the large, single standard carnations; the spray carnations, in which I include pinks; the micro, which are miniature plants; and the well-known Sweet Williams. Spray carnations alone are available in over 60 colours, and carnations as a whole can be grown and bought in an infinite number of markings and shades. Alas, carnations are among the flowers which are most commonly dyed, so they can even be found in blue and green. However, I hasten to add that a new variety is now available which is white tinged with green and, like all other green flowers, is expected to become a favourite among those who are continually searching for something new and different.

Generally, carnations are strong and reliable flowers which can last for up to three weeks given the right care. They are easy to condition: with a sharp pair of scissors, cut off at least 1 inch (2.5 cm) of stem between the nodes (the point where leaves or buds emerge from the stem) to encourage water absorption. Specialist foods are available for carnations, but a standard flower-food will suffice. Occasionally, you may find the words "post-harvest treated" on a box of carnations, which means that the flowers have undergone treatment after picking to prolong their vase life.

Although carnations are cultivated throughout the year, the best buys are those grown with the benefit of natural sunlight. This is a rule that can be applied to all types of flowers,

Left: Basket arrangements are given a vibrant and fresh look by selecting a brightly coloured basket and using clashing colours such as red and orange carnations with rose hips (*Rosa canina*), *Viburnum* berries, *Helenium*, hops (*Humulus*), *Crocosmia* seed heads and strongly coloured foliage. The burgundy *Cotinus* leaves and the lime-coloured, furry *Amaranthus* help to make the overall effect rich and sumptuous.

Above: The spray carnation 'Sorentino', cream carnation 'Roma' and 'Kortina Chanel' carnations are mixed with 'Mainzer Fastnach'

roses (*Rosa*), *Sedum*, *Nigella* seed heads, *Astrantia* and burgundy 'Arabian Night' dahlias (*Dahlia*) in a heart-shaped, copper cake tin.

Right top: Make a scented topiary centre piece by filling a wire frame with floral foam and then arranging some border carnations,

or pinks as they are commonly known. The two used in this arrangement are the popular pinks 'Doris' and 'Haytor'. These carnations have

an aromatic scent and therefore mix well with the herb rue (*Ruta*), which is excellent for flower arrangements because it lasts well in water

and floral foam. The strawberries were placed into the floral foam with cocktail sticks so they could be removed, washed and eaten later.

Right bottom: One of my favourite carnations is 'Charmeur', an adorable jewel-like purple. Here I placed it with the clove-coloured

carnation 'Scia', plus 'Dark Pierrot' and 'Oliver'. I used heavy reeds swirled through the arrangement and *Eucomis bicolor* on the top.

and follows the same logic that most people use when buying fruit and vegetables: strawberries and tomatoes grown all year around may look good but their flavour is lost unless they are cultivated with the correct amount of sunlight. Carnations grown in bleak northern winter conditions may have weak stems and are more likely to snap than those grown in warmer, sunnier climes. However, there are some exceptions to this rule, and commercial growers are continually trying to develop stronger varieties such as 'Nora', the most frequently cultivated pink carnation which has very pretty, fluted petals and excellent stamina.

One area where carnations come into their own is bridal work. Their longevity means they are highly suitable for arrangements that have to be made in advance or will be left in high temperatures at a wedding reception. Carnation buttonholes can be made the day before a wedding, and will last well even if they are wired. Before they became so highly developed, it was common to "feather" spray carnations, which involved removing the petals from their calyx and wiring them together in groups for wedding arrangements. I like to use micro carnations in pomanders for bridesmaids to hold, and find spray carnations useful for topiary trees and balls, which are often requested for weddings, because they last such a long time.

The cream standard carnation may be considered to be an uninspiring flower, but it is very good at covering floral foam and filling arrangements. As it is economical to buy, it can be used as a base flower with other, more exotic blooms added to enhance the arrangement. A useful rule to remember when you are buying flowers for arrangements is to choose an appropriate or favourite flower, then select inexpensive blooms that are good fillers and, finally, flowers which are in season.

L I L I E S

These refined, sophisticated flowers have been popular throughout history and are still favourites in today's

cosmopolitan world. They suit contemporary and traditional arrangements, and can be dressed up or down.

There is a vast range of lilies (*Lilium*), from star-shaped to trumpet-shaped, and they grow in a number of

colours, some plain, some striped and some spotted. However, for many people the quintessential lily is

white. It is an emblem of majesty and purity, and is thought to have been in existence since the beginning

of the Ice Age. This lily is often associated with religious festivals, and for the past 2,000 years white lilies

have been depicted with the Virgin Mary in paintings by a great many artists.

Left: A bud of the hybrid developed from the scented *Lilium auratum*. This white variety is 'Pompeii', is very strong and has massive, star-shaped flowers.

Above, from left to right: The beautiful, very pale, spotted 'La Reve'; the highly sought-after, pure white 'Casablanca'; the pink 'Laura'.

Right: This single-headed variety of *Lilium longiflorum* has been specially bred for flower arrangements. Here it is combined with snake grass (*Scirpus tabernaemontani* 'Zebrinus'), *Yucca* tips, bear grass (*Dasylirion*), *Sedum* flowerheads, papyrus (*Cyperus papyrus*) and *Cyclamen* leaves.

The lily is also a symbol of the Resurrection and as such is closely associated with Easter. It is often the longiflorum lily (*L. longiflorum*) that is placed upon altars after the four weeks of Lent when churches are left undecorated. This flower is also known as the Madonna lily and it was taken to England by the Romans. The Madonna lily was originally transported to England because of the therapeutic qualities of its sap, which was believed to relieve pain in the feet of soldiers after their long marches.

The original hybrid *L. candidum* has largely been replaced by *L. longiflorum*, which literally means "long-flowered". The best longiflorum lily is 'White Europe'. The quality of longiflorum lilies varies considerably, and often what seems to be a bargain when you buy it can later prove to be a disappointment. The best lilies will last for at least ten days and are heavily perfumed. They can be purchased when still in green bud and will open into white flowers with yellow stamens. There are normally about three flowerheads to a stem, although some produce as many as seven. However, it is unlikely that the smaller green heads will ever open in water.

The botanists who gathered lilies from all over the world have bequeathed us a rich

heritage. One of my favourite lilies, *L. regale*, was discovered comparatively

recently. The British plant-hunter, Dr Ernest Wilson, found this lily in

Western China in 1937. It was growing, he wrote: "not in twos and threes

but in hundreds, in thousands, aye, in tens of thousands." He sent some

to a British nursery where they were tested and found to do very well in

British soil. Dr Wilson was sent to collect further bulbs and slipped on some granite,

which left him forever with what he referred to as his "lily limp". Quantities of these bulbs

reached the United States at about the same time, which is when the American love affair with lilies

began. These spectacular lilies will grow to 3 feet (1 metre) and can carry as many as 14 trumpets on

their stems. Their scent is divine, and their wine and pink markings are most attractive. The centres of these lilies are almost a

buttercup yellow and it is from this strain that the golden yellow 'Royal Gold' variety (*see pages 34–5*) was developed.

Another spectacular lily is *L. auratum*, which has yellow stripes. It has a delicious scent

and bears either crimson or gold spots. *L. auratum* is the thoroughbred from which a

whole group of scented lilies known as *L. speciosum* were developed. These beau-

tiful, large lilies often grow on stems at least 3 feet (1 metre) long and they

have huge flowerheads which open to produce a most heady fragrance.

They are available all the year around, but are at their peak in

September and October and scarce at the beginning of the year.

Often they can be purchased in tight bud, and they will last for 14

days. Removing the stamens can help the flowers to last

even longer, as they may be tricked into continuing to

flower in the vain hope of being fertilized. In addition,

this prevents the flower from being stained by its pollen.

Hybridizers all over the world are working on new

varieties, and one of the most recent lilies to be sold

as a cut flower is the wonderful 'Casablanca', which

has such large, star-shaped flowerheads that they often

Left: The large heads of lilies provide good focal points for mixed bunches. This summer combination includes 'La Reve' lilies, snapdragons (*Antirrhinum*), white *Trachelium*, pale pink *Bouvardia* and the Peruvian lily (*Alstroemeria*). Plaited South African grass is looped through the flowers.

Bottom left: A front-facing arrangement of *Lilium rubrum* and white 'Star Gazer' lilies. The shape is traditional but the foliage is unusual – bulrushes (*Typha*), papyrus (*Cyperus papyrus*) and arum lily (*Zantedeschia*) leaves.

snap their stems. They are popular because of their extreme longevity and their lovely fragrance. However, they are expensive and are often priced according to the number of flowerheads which are borne on each stem. A stronger hybrid, with more erect and much sturdier stems, has been developed from this strain and is called 'Pompeii'.

The Asian hybrids are usually smaller and less expensive. They grow in a vast range of colours – the white 'Sterling Star'; the cream 'Mont Blanc'; the yellow 'Connecticut King'; the salmon pink 'Montreux'; the orange 'Enchantment'; the red 'Monte Negro'; the burgundy 'America'; and the dark pink 'La Toya', to name a few. The stems can be up to 3 feet (1 metre) long. The lilies are graded by the length of stem and number of flowerheads. They are available all year around and comprise about 60 percent of the lily market. When purchasing these lilies, look for stems where the lower three buds are showing colour. Condition them as you would other lilies – trim at least 1 inch (2.5 cm) off the stems, remove the stamens, leave in water and flower-food overnight and arrange them in more water and flower-food. Remove faded flowers whenever necessary. These flowers will easily last for a week, and sometimes for up to 14 days.

Above: A two-tier spring arrangement of 'Pompeii' lilies with catkins (*Salix*), blue hyacinths (*Hyacinthus*), Israeli lupins (*Lupinus*) and *Lysimachia*. The bright green guelder roses (*Viburnum opulus*) and laurustinus (*V. tinus*) are perfect spring fillers.

A R U M   L I

Right: The calla lily (*Zantedeschia*) has a timeless beauty and elegance and was popularized by the Art Nouveau movement.

Above, from left to right: Sometimes the golden arum lily (*Z. elliottiana*) is deformed, with two flowerheads per stem; a perfect specimen of the golden arum lily; the arum lily (*Z. aethiopica* 'Tinkerbell') is white splashed with green; the pink arum lily (*Z. rehmannii*), unlike most coloured arum lilies whose leaves are spotted, has unmarked green leaves.

Commonly known as arum or calla lilies (*Zantedeschia*), these striking flowers have a timeless and classic appearance that is perfectly suited to formal and informal, traditional and contemporary situations. Originally from Africa, the white varieties are by far the most common of all the arum lilies, and are the traditional choice for decorating churches throughout the Christian world. A symbol of purity, they have often been chosen for the most poignant occasions in life and are popular with brides because of their supreme elegance, simplicity and beauty. Arum lilies have also long been used for sympathy tributes, particularly in the United Kingdom so, unfortunately, for many people they symbolize sad occasions. Therefore, they are not always good choices for gifts, particularly if the recipient is elderly.

LIES

BRIDAL BOUQUET WITH ARUM LILIES

MATERIALS

Large mirror

7 arum lilies (*Zantedeschia aethiopica*)

Jasmine (*Jasminum polyanthum*) trails

3 *Ligularia tussilaginea* leaves

Plastic tie, string or raffia

Silk ribbon

1 This is a simple tied bunch that can be created for a bride or as an over-the-arm hostess bouquet suitable for presentation to a ballerina or other performer. It will last out of water for several hours. The advantage of creating a bouquet like this, rather than a traditional wired spray bouquet, is that you can construct it at the last minute and even transport it in water. You may find a large mirror useful when you make the bouquet because it will help you to see the flowers from the front while you assemble them. Make sure that the *Ligularia* leaves are shiny by rubbing them with a damp cloth. Begin with a pointed arum lily, a sprig of jasmine and one *Ligularia* leaf. The jasmine may be purchased as a cut flower or as a plant and should be conditioned well in water and flower-food before it is used for this bouquet. The

leaf will provide a background to the flowers and also offer them protection. Loosely wrap the plastic tie, string or raffia around the stems.

2 Place two arum lilies so they point outward alongside the first one you positioned, then add some more trails of jasmine. Position another leaf on the left-hand side of the arrangement. Loosely bind the stems again.

3 Continue to add the arum lilies, checking the arrangement in the mirror so that you can place each flower to its best advantage. Choose a leaf that points upward and position it to hide from view the area that you will be tying. Bind around the stems with the plastic tie or string, then fasten.

Trim the stems and place in water until the celebration. Tie the silk ribbon in a lavish bow which will hide the binding around the stems (*right*).

Opposite: Always consider the colour of the container when choosing your flowers, as in this simple but dramatic arrangement of arum lilies, witch hazel (*Hamamelis mollis*) and the flowers and leaves of *Calathea crocata*, usually seen as a houseplant.

Left: A country-style arrangement uses arum lilies with *Celastrus orbiculatus*, *Curcuma*, ornamental maize (*Zea mays*) and zebra grass (*Miscanthus sinensis* 'Zebrinus'). The cylindrical vase is covered with corrugated brown paper and tied with raffia for a rustic look.

Both the flowers and the big, heart-shaped leaves of the arum lily have appealed to twentieth-century designers and artists, in particular to the followers of the Art Nouveau movement which was in its heyday at the beginning of the century. Artists and craftsmen incorporated the flower's pods, tendrils and leaves in their designs, and lily motifs were repeated endlessly on furniture and silverware. These artists were fascinated by the curvy spathes (bracts) which carry the lily's tiny flowers. If you grow the tubers for yourself, or appreciate these lilies as cut flowers, it is easy to understand the designers' fascination with these plants. Today, arum lilies are still very popular with designers, artists, photographers and architects, and are often chosen as gifts for men because of their strong and unfussy shapes. They are also particularly suited for ikebana (the Japanese art of flower arranging), which involves a number of complex rules and requires a great attention to detail when arranging the flowers.

The cuckoo pint (*Arum italicum*) is a variety of arum lily grown for its seed heads, which are very useful for floral decoration. The green and orange spadix is like a stick with masses of pea-shaped berries arranged in a linear cluster at the end. These plants grow naturally in temperate climates and can often be seen in the wild. They originate from South America and Southern Europe, hence their botanical name that means "from Italy". They are largely cultivated by the Dutch now and are available in small boxes. Order them in advance because you will not find them in flower shops. The seed heads are only available in limited numbers between June and October, and they are at their peak between July and September. Trim the stems and condition them in the normal way, adding a drop of bleach to their water to prevent bacterial attack to which they are susceptible. The seed heads last for up to 20 days. The berries and seed heads are poisonous and should be kept out of the reach of children.

T U L I P S

Tulips (*Tulipa gesneriana*) are the stalwarts of temperate gardens, surviving underground over the winter months

to flower faithfully in gardens and parks from early spring. Universally loved for their brilliant splashes of

colour, tulips are plentiful and inexpensive as cut flowers. When the gardeners of the northern hemisphere

are preparing to plant their autumn bulbs, tulips are sprouting in Australia; the bulb industry is also very

large on the west coast of Japan. These esteemed flowers have been celebrated by artists and craftsmen

alike as an emblem or feature of design for ceramics and porcelain, and they have also appeared in many

fine paintings. Four hundred years of growers' skill and enthusiasm have produced an enormous assortment

of cut tulip flowers and the period of availability each year is lengthening.

Left: *Tulipa* 'Flaming Parrot'. "Broken" tulips like this one, which were popular in the seventeenth century, were generally

referred to as Rembrandt tulips after the artist who painted his wife Saskia with such a tulip dangling from her ear.

Now known as parrot tulips, these flowers, with their striped and curly edges, are enjoying a revival today.

Above, from left to right: The red lily-flowering 'Aladdin'; pale pink double-flowering 'Angelique'; pink, late-flowering

'Miss Piggy'; pink and green, late-flowering viridiflora 'Artist'; crimson and green parrot tulip 'Black Parrot'.

Left: Parrot tulips, known in Holland as parakeet tulips, have full, heavy heads which cannot always support themselves so their stems droop and twist. The variety shown here is 'Estella Rijnveld' which illustrates the "broken" pattern very clearly.

Right: A vase of tulips arranged in groups to show off each variety's distinctive colour and form. From left to right: 'Yokohama'; 'Aladdin'; 'White Dream' dyed blue by being left in blue-coloured water; 'Hamilton'; 'Aladdin' and 'Monte Carlo'.

PEONY TULIPS IN A LEAF-COVERED VASE

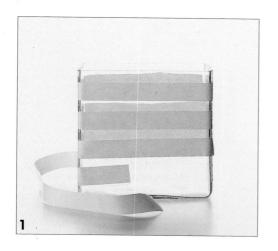

MATERIALS

Glass container

Double-sided adhesive tape

Calathea veitchiana leaves

Sharp knife and/or scissors

Length of raffia

Lady's mantle (*Alchemilla mollis*)

Hypericum (*Hypericum*) berries

Birch (*Betula*) twigs

Red peony tulips (*Tulipa*)

1 Take a square glass container and wrap some long strips of double-sided adhesive tape around all four sides until they are completely covered. Instead, you could use a glass jar or a large plastic container because it will be completely hidden by the leaves.

2 Select *Calathea* leaves of a similar size, shape and marking and which are all in good condition. Discard any leaves which are torn or show signs of insect damage. Cut the bottom of the

leaves to produce a straight edge to align with the base of the container. Begin to stick the leaves onto the container, with the edges overlapping and the tips of the leaves pointing upward. Make sure that all the container's glass is hidden. Tie the length of raffia around the middle of the container in a firm knot; trim the ends.

3 Fill the container with water; it is simpler to do this now rather than later. Arrange the foliage, then cut some birch twigs into short lengths and add them to the arrangement.

4 Add the multi-petalled peony tulips, arranging them evenly among the foliage. Use a few more sprigs of lady's mantle to fill any gaps.

To complete the display, add a few longer-length birch twigs (*right*) in order to give the arrangement extra height and shape.

Tulips continue to grow after they are cut and placed in water, so there are times when you have arranged them only to return the next day and find they have marched a whole head above their fellow flowers and foliage. They also have a tendency to move toward the light, so tulip arrangements may need daily adjustment. A site with even lighting suits them best.

Above: A summer posy with a pink and purple theme. I arranged pretty button-like daisies (*Bellis*) and violas around double pink 'Daladier' tulips. The flowers are set off with guelder roses (*Viburnum opulus*), whitebeam (*Sorbus*) and huckleberry leaves (*Gaylussacia*); to break up the rigid outline.

Right top: 'Ad Rem', 'Monte Carlo' and 'Apricot' tulips are mixed with *Narcissus* and bunches of *Muscari*, *Myosotis* and stripy *Ranunculus*.

Right bottom: You can take your colour theme from the variations in one flower. The 'Allegretto' tulip is red with a yellow tip and here I have used foliage and flowers that bring out these colours – wallflowers (*Cheiranthus*), spurge (*Euphorbia*), *Hypericum* and *Leucadendron* 'Sunset' encircled in *Galax* leaves.

Although tulips were originally grown in the royal gardens of the Ottoman Empire, they derive their name from a Persian word meaning "turban-covered head", which is a picturesque description of their distinctive shape. The flowers were much admired in Europe and they became an instant and immense success in the middle of the seventeenth century, culminating in "tulipomania" (1634–7) when bulbs changed hands for preposterous sums. One feature of tulip bulbs which caused this early obsession was their tendency, during cross-breeding, to "break" and form a new colour and new markings. This "broken" characteristic, which we now know is caused by a viral infection, stunned these early collectors. Dealers were prepared to stake their entire fortunes on a few tulip bulbs which were traded like stocks and shares on the stock markets of London and Amsterdam. All the while everyone was making a fat profit, the boom flourished. However, the market crashed in spectacular fashion in 1637 and some dealers' lives were completely ruined by insolvency and bankruptcy.

Tulips should be bought, or cut from the garden, when their buds are showing colour. To condition them, cut at least 1 inch (2.5 cm) from the stems with a sharp pair of scissors and strip the lower foliage. If the tulips are very limp, wrap them up in a couple of sheets of newspaper, tie the bundle with string to hold the flowers upright and then plunge them into a solution of flower-food and warm water. Leave them like this for about 12 hours before arranging them in more flower-food and water. Top up the containers frequently because tulips are heavy drinkers. They should last in water for between five and eight days.

Tulips mix well with other spring flowers, although if you are using them with daffodils (*Narcissi*) you must condition these first in a separate vase otherwise the slime exuded from their stems will ruin the tulips. Tulips are very popular flowers for posies and I have shown them here in a number of different colour-ways. They are not usually fragrant, although some – such as the sturdy, bright orange 'Ad Rem', the double bright yellow 'Monte Carlo' and the deep red parrot tulip 'Rococo' – have subtle perfumes.

Tulips are generally classified under the season in which they would traditionally have flowered. The first to bloom are known as "early-flowering tulips", and are a cross between *T. gesneriana*, which was originally from Iran, and the plant *T. suaveolens* from Asia Minor. These tulips were once of great economic importance because they flowered early, but now other cultivar groups can also be brought to flower early. Mid-season species such as 'Bing Crosby' have longer stems and larger flowers, and the most popular cultivar is 'Apricot Beauty'. The late-blooming tulips are the most interesting varieties and include lily-flowered tulips such as the red, spiky 'Aladdin'. The most stylish and elegant tulips are cultivated in the South of France and are renowned for their stems, which are often over 12 inches (30 cm) long. This strong variety is usually sold by the stem and is rarely affordable in a bunch, but it does last very well and is useful for arrangements which call for tall flowers. 'Flaming Parrot' is an example of this variety and is shown on the facing page.

Parrot tulips traditionally flower later in the season and another late-flowering tulip which is worth a special mention is the fringed variety, with jagged and fringed petals. The pale pink 'Fancy Frills' and the yellow 'Hamilton' are the most commonly available fringed varieties. Recently, a new class of tulip called viridiflora has taken supremacy over the late-flowering varieties. These flowers are particularly popular in floral decoration because the tulips have unusual markings and are characterized by a green band along the length of each petal. New varieties of this tulip are being developed every day but 'Artist', which is apricot, is one of the prettiest. Double tulips are highly sought-after; one of the most popular of all tulips is 'Angelique' which, although a late-flowering double tulip, has been adapted by the Dutch to flower throughout their season. It is also a very popular choice for growing at home in borders and containers.

Tulips which are grown commercially for their bulbs have to be cut when they come into flower so that all the goodness will be directed back into the bulb. However, the cut heads are not wasted, because they are used in marvellous flower festivals which often feature huge floats covered with the flowerheads in all sorts of designs. Spalding is the home of the flower festival in the United Kingdom and similar events are held all over the world each spring.

Above: Ivy (*Hedera*) berries and guelder roses (*Viburnum opulus*) are mixed with scabious (*Scabiosa*), 'Angelique' tulips and 'Diadeen' roses (*Rosa*).

Right: This is an arrangement of 'Flaming Parrot' tulips, the long-stemmed flowers which are grown in the South of France.

CHRYSAN

Right: A large-flowered single chrysanthemum, 'Autumn Days', commonly referred to as a "bloom".

Above, from left to right: This versatile white daisy chrysanthemum is known as 'Cassa', which is available all the year around; the acid-green chrysanthemum bloom which is called 'Shamrock'; blooms are described by the shape of their heads – this one, 'Brietner', is a reflexed chrysanthemum because its petals form an umbrella-like outline.

The chrysanthemum (*Chrysanthemum*) has been grown in the Far East for over 2,000 years. It is the national flower of Japan and so admired that even the Emperor's Chrysanthemum Throne bears its name. "Chrysanthemum" comes from the Greek words *chrysos*, which means "gold", and *anthemon*, which means "a flower". The original species was yellow, but today chrysanthemums are grown in almost every shade. They are herbaceous bushes and can be cultivated under glass or outdoors. Both the single bloom and the cluster grow from one stalk; it is the cluster variety which we refer to as a spray and which is grown most often. All these chrysanthemums are classified as *C. indicum* and belong to the Compositae family.

T H E M U M S

Although the chrysanthemum arrived in the Netherlands via its trade routes with the Dutch East Indies, the flower once grew in the imperial gardens of China. However, it is impossible to say whether the plant originated there or in Japan. Each year, on the ninth day of the ninth month, Japan holds a national festival devoted to the chrysanthemum, in which the flower is honoured as a symbol of longevity. It is depicted on the Japanese flag and on its imperial weapons, and the Order of the Chrysanthemum is the highest imperial honour which one can receive in Japan.

Chrysanthemums are the florists' most useful flowers and they are extremely versatile, practical and serviceable. They are among the top five most cultivated and popular flowers in the world. In Japan, the United Kingdom, the United States and the Netherlands, more chrysanthemums are sold than any other cut flower, and it is in these countries that most of the developments in the species have been made. These flowers are represented in all kinds of floristry and all types of flower arranging, from the very simple to the large and extravagant. Chrysanthemums grow in every colour except blue, but the Dutch will dye them that colour if asked. Certain colours are more popular in particular seasons – red and orange are good for autumn or fall and for Christmas, while white and yellow are more popular at Easter.

Left: This formal topiary tree was made from a floral foam ball impaled on three sticks pushed into a small urn of floral foam. Elegant, simple white chrysanthemums were based in the foam (*see pages 16–17*). Interest has been added by twining clematis (*Clematis*) vine down the trunk.

Chrysanthemums are used to mark the milestones in our lives, from happy occasions, such as weddings, to very sad ones, such as funerals. In some countries, including France, these flowers are viewed quite simply as funeral flowers and therefore are not deemed suitable as gifts.

Chrysanthemums are available throughout the year, thanks to special greenhouses which constantly provide the exact amount of daylight they need in order to produce flower buds. This year-round cultivation, which originated in the United States, is now used in all flower-growing regions. It requires a combination of computer technology, agricultural science and an extraordinary amount of labour to bring these flowers to our markets all the year around.

Of all flowers, chrysanthemums are easily the most hybridized. They are divided into their most popular forms of disbudded and non-disbudded. The single-headed disbudded type is often referred to as a "bloom". These flowers are the traditional garden flowers grown for their prized blooms and often entered in horticultural competitions. The single flowerhead is over 4 inches (10 cm) across and appears at the end of a single stem that can be as long as 2 feet (60 cm). These blooms are excellent for large arrangements and make good, inexpensive focal flowers for church pedestals and for harvest and Thanksgiving dinners. For a while, these large flowers lost their popularity, but they are now making a comeback, and new colours are being developed to tempt people to buy them. The acid-green 'Shamrock' bloom (*see page* 56) is currently very popular, as are other green flowers.

Above: Recently, a number of micro chrysanthemums (santini type) have been developed. The double green pompon is 'Kermit' and the red daisy is 'Reginette', mixed with dahlias (*Dahlia*) and *Galax* leaves as foliage.

Another variety, which is called 'Inga', looks like a fried egg. Its yellow centre is encircled by white petals, but I prefer to use daisy-style chrysanthemums for the same effect. The cream 'Fred Shoesmith' and the golden 'Rivalry' are both excellent and are described as incurved chrysanthemums because their blooms are the shape of a perfect globe. My favourite shape is reflexed, which is flatter and not quite as globular. The popular two-tone rust chrysanthemum 'Tom Pearce' belongs to this category.

Spray or bunch chrysanthemums are the non-disbudded type and grow in an astonishing range of colours and styles. The flowers appear at the end of small branches that are borne from a single stem. There are between five and nine

Right: An alternative to using the traditional autumnal or fall colours of orange and gold is to use burgundy and other wine-coloured chrysanthemums mixed with white and mauve double spray asters (*Aster*), artichoke (*Cynara*) flowers, trailing love-lies-bleeding (*Amaranthus*), pink nerines (*Nerine*), liguster privet (*Ligustrum*) berries, ivy (*Hedera*) berries and lichen-covered larch (*Larix*) twigs.

Opposite: The ornamental cabbage is an inexpensive filler for an autumnal or fall centre piece. Ornamental gourds and 'Shamrock' chrysanthemums have been placed singly, whereas the spray chrysanthemums 'Purple Pennine Wine', 'Dark Flamenco' and 'Gompie Geel' have been placed in groups of three. The conical frame is made from moss and wire mesh and the trunk is wired in place.

heads per stem and the flowers are at their heaviest during their natural season in the autumn or fall. There are many types within this general category and this form currently comprises about 90 percent of all chrysanthemums sold.

Within the spray cultivars there are also some other groups. The spider spray chrysanthemum is feathery, light and shaggy. The two classic spider chrysanthemums are 'White Spider' and 'Yellow Spider'. Occasionally you can buy pompon flowers on a spray. These flowers are excellent for basing, which is the floristry term for cutting flowerheads short and massing them together (*see pages 16–17*), and are often featured in sympathy work around the world.

Decorative chrysanthemums include a massive group of flowers, many of which are semi-double or daisy-like in shape. The pyrethrums (*Tanacetum*), or anemone-flowered chrysanthemums, belong to this group. They are universally popular and mix well with many other flowers.

Chrysanthemums are extremely long-lasting and should bloom for between seven and fourteen days, if not more. The foliage dies before the flowers so this should be continually removed and the stems recut. Not so long ago it was believed that the stems of chrysanthemums should be crushed with a wooden mallet. However, this is entirely the wrong way to condition them because it allows bacteria to enter the stems and reduces the flowers' intake of water. All you need do is cut at least 1 inch (2.5 cm) off the stems and remove all the lower foliage, then condition the flowers in water and flower-food. These flowers work well in floral foam, are inexpensive, tough, wire easily and keep extraordinarily well, so are good flowers to experiment with. They are extremely sensitive to the ageing hormone, present in ethylene gas, and also emit large amounts of it themselves, so it is best to keep them in a cool environment during the conditioning process and away from other sensitive flowers.

BRIDESMAID'S CHRYSANTHEMUM POMANDER

MATERIALS

Block of floral foam or a ball of foam

Sharp knife

Silky piping cord

Heavy florist's stub wires

Pair of sharp scissors

Flowering gardenia (*Gardenia*) plant

Ivy (*Hedera*) berries

Blue scabious (*Scabiosa caucasia*
  'Clive Greaves')

Cornflowers (*Centaurea*)

'Cassa' chrysanthemum
  (*Chrysanthemum indicum*)

1 If you cannot buy a small floral foam ball, carve a block of floral foam into a sphere. Soak the foam in water until the air bubbles stop rising to the surface. You should never force foam underwater – allow it to sink slowly so that water can be taken up evenly throughout the foam. Do not reuse old floral foam because it never regains its initial absorbency. Pin the middle of the piping cord into the bottom of the ball with some hairpin or bobby pin wires, then bring the cord up around the ball, tie it in a firm knot, then return the cord down the other two sides of the ball and knot firmly, as if you were wrapping up a gift. Secure the knot in place with more hairpin wires. Knot the two ends of the cord to make a loop by which the pomander can be carried. The cord will get wet and messy so choose a

dark colour. Hang up the ball so you can work on it from all sides.

2 Taking small 2-inch (5-cm) sprigs of gardenia foliage and ivy, cover all the floral foam to create a rounded shape.

3 Cut the flowers from the gardenia plant and place them deep in the floral foam. Cut down the scabious and cornflower heads and arrange them around the ball, being very careful to hold the stems as close to the foam as possible to prevent them snapping.

Cut the flowerheads from a spray of daisy chrysanthemums and position them throughout the arrangement (*right*). There is such an infinite variety of spray chrysanthemums available that you could use them in virtually any colourway you wish. They are always in season and are inexpensive, which makes them an excellent choice for novice flower arrangers.

Left: The *Paphiopedilum* varieties, which are available between September and January, have the most peculiar appearance of all orchids, so need to be arranged with care. This example is *P.* x *Maudiae*, an early nineteenth-century hybrid.

Above, from left to right: *Cattleya* orchids, such as this *C. trianae*, are useful for corsages and wired wedding work; my favourite orchids are *Phalaenopsis*; there are over 600 species of *Oncidium* orchids, which makes it difficult to identify and specify them; the *Dendrobium* orchids, like this *D.* 'Robin', are commercially grown and exported from Thailand.

O R C H I D S

Orchids are the most passionately cultivated flowers in the world. For centuries, their different varieties, sizes, shapes, guises and even fragrances have attracted enthusiasts, plant lovers and collectors. As cut flowers, orchids have long been symbols for the exotic and mysterious and signify romance, extravagance and the desire for intimacy. They grow in nearly every country of the world and in every climate, with the exception of Arctic and desert regions. Orchids are some of the most bizarre and diverse plants on earth, and they grow in virtually every colour and every shape. They are also masters of sexual deception – they imitate bees and wasps so that the male insects try to mate with the flowers and, in doing so, pollinate them.

Left: The pretty lilac *Vanda rothschildiana*, shown growing in a small crate, is a beautiful cut flower and houseplant.

Right: My favourite orchid, both as a flowering plant and a cut flower, is the moth orchid (*Phalaenopsis*), shown here with screw pine (*Pandanus*) foliage.

Orchids are perennial flowering plants belonging to the genus Orchidaceae. This is a gargantuan family which has as many as 30,000 species and more than 80,000 hybrids. Such vast numbers makes it the most superior flowering plant family in the world, much larger than the sunflower family of Compositae, and even larger than the huge grass family of Gramineae. Since the first artificial hybrid was registered in Britain in the mid-nineteenth century, the number of hybrids has increased each day because the species are so compatible with one another and there are so many fanatical orchid growers ever keen to experiment and create new hybrids.

Orchids are as diverse in fragrance as they are in shape and colour, and the perfumes vary from the scent of coconuts, cinnamon and bitter almonds to some pungent and quite unpleasant odours of rotting cheese and decaying meat. Despite this variation in fragrance, orchids have always been symbols of opulence and courtship. The cattleya (*Cattleya*) orchid is one of the classic corsage flowers. Of all the orchids, cattleyas have the shortest life as cut flowers and will only survive for six or seven days. They need constant warmth.

BRIDESMAID'S ORCHID CIRCLET

MATERIALS

2 stems of miniature *Cymbidium* orchids

Selection of florist's wires

Green florist's tape

Clematis (*Clematis*) or similar vines

Ivy (*Hedera*) trails

Coordinating ribbon

1 Remove the miniature *Cymbidium* flowers from the stems and carefully insert a silver wire up a stem. Take another wire and push it through the stem at the base of the flower.

2 Bend the wire like a hairpin or bobby pin around the stem. Leave one leg of the wire hanging down the stem, then wind the other leg around the stem and the first wire three times.

3 Take a strip of green florist's tape and wrap it around the stem to hide the wires. This tape also helps to strengthen the stem and seal in moisture. Repeat this process with the other *Cymbidium* florets.

4 Twist the dried vines into an informal wreath and bind them together with some heavy reel wire. Any type of vine, such as honeysuckle, can be used instead of clematis, and it is wise to collect or buy this in the autumn or fall when it is bare of leaves.

5 Twist ivy trails through the vine to create a wonderfully lush effect. There is no need to secure the ivy trails with wires – they will be pulled through the pieces of vine and held tight in this way. Select ivy that has undamaged leaves and wash it if it is dirty.

For this circlet, I used two varieties of miniature *Cymbidium* orchids – the dark red 'Pink Perfection' and the green 'Greenland'. Arrange the wired orchids around the wreath (*right*), with each wire twisted through the vines. When each floret is secured, cut off any excess wire to prevent it causing any damage. Take care to place the green and red orchids at random around the wreath, bearing in mind that the circlet will be viewed from all angles. Leave a space at the top for a ribbon and thread it through the vine, then tie it in a knot to make a firm loop by which it can be carried.

The cymbidium (*Cymbidium*) orchid is one of the most successful commercial varieties, the most widely available and probably the best known. Cymbidiums are popular as flowers for corsages and are by far the best orchids for wiring, which is why I chose to show the lovely green and red varieties in the wired bridesmaid's circlet (*see pages 68–9*).

Some of the flowers known as Singapore orchids belong to the dendrobium (*Dendrobium*) family. The purple 'Madame Pompadour' and the white 'Madame Pompadour Wit' are both popular with brides. 'James Storei' is the most popular variety of all because it survives in water for at least two weeks and is a long-lasting complement to Christmas foliage and berries. The oncidium (*Oncidium*) family is also very popular for cut flowers, and the yellow 'Golden Shower' variety is the most common. It is possible to buy these flowers all year around, although their best season is from January to March. They last for up to fifteen days and are exported with their stems enclosed in a phial of water and flower-food. Some orchids, such as the paphiopedilum (*Paphiopedilum*) varieties, which are available between September and January, have the strangest colours and shapes. These orchids are remarkable for their detailed markings, lines and spots. They are such unique flowers that they should be used with extreme care in arrangements and are best admired on their own. They have to be arranged carefully because of their short stems.

To condition all orchids, cut at least 1 inch (2.5 cm) off the stems at an angle with a pair of scissors, then place them in a solution of flower-food and warm water. The stems of orchids should never be allowed to dry out, which is why they are transported in water. Generally speaking, cut orchids which have already been arranged benefit if a small piece of stem is cut off at an angle every few days and they are given fresh water and flower-food. This procedure improves their intake of water and so extends the lives of the flowers. If an orchid becomes limp, you can replace its lost moisture by immersing the whole flower in tepid water for about half an hour – you will be amazed at the way that the flower's sepals and petals revive.

Left: This container has been covered with *Calathea veitchiana* leaves, as shown on page 50. Inside the vase is the very popular *Dendrobium* 'Madame Pompadour' mixed with a variety of other striped orchids. The tall pink spikes are the flowering banana (*Musa ornata*), which matches the orchids.

Above: A mixture of *Dendrobium* 'James Storei', the stripy tiger variety known as 'Maggie Oei' and the orange 'Tangerine'.

ANT

H U R I U M S

Left: Anthuriums grow in a range of different markings and colours.

This one, *Anthurium* 'Meringue', has a cream spathe and a pink spadix.

Above, from left to right: A. 'Greenpeace'; A. 'Avoclaudia'; A. 'Fantasia'.

These exotic, long-lasting heart-shaped flowers originate from the rain forests of Colombia, although they are now cultivated in most flower-growing regions of the world and are available throughout the year because they travel well. The Dutch grow anthuriums (*Anthurium*), commonly referred to as "painter's palette" flowers, all year around and, when in season, they are available from the South Pacific and West Indies. Most anthuriums sold in the United States and Japan are grown in Hawaii, which has over 80 commercial growers. The most common varieties of anthurium are *A. andraeanum* hybrids, which are the ones shown in this chapter, and the flamingo flower (*A. scherzerianum*) which is grown as a flowering houseplant. The perfect shape and colour of some varieties make them ideal for clean-lined arrangements.

Right: Anthuriums are such strong flowers in colour and form that they look marvellous arranged on their own. The anthuriums used here are 'Cuba' and 'Midori', with Arabian chincherinchees (*Ornithogalum thyrsoides*) and arum lily (*Zantedeschia*) leaves.

CANDELABRA WITH SWEET PEAS AND FRUIT

MATERIALS

Candelabra

3 candles

Floral foam adhesive

Punnet of red currants

1 plastic candle-cup

Floral foam tape

Floral foam

Galax leaves

Hebe leaves

Eucalyptus gunnii leaves

Senecio (*Senecio*)

Cherries and grapes

'Baccarolla' roses (*Rosa*)

'Black Tea' roses

Sweet peas (*Lathyrus odorata*)

1 Firmly place your candles in the holders, using a floral foam adhesive. Arrange a selection of red currants around the base of each holder.

2 In the central candle-holder, fix a plastic candle-cup, available from florists, and secure with floral foam tape. Fill it with wet floral foam that has been soaked thoroughly in a solution of tepid water and flower-food. Establish the outline of your arrangement with *Galax*, *Hebe*, eucalyptus and senecio foliage. The gray hues of these leaves suits perfectly the silvery candelabra which I used here. A bronze or copper one would look good with richer, darker foliage.

3 Wire small groups of cherries by pushing florist's wire through them to make a hairpin or bobby pin, then place them in the floral foam. Add the roses. As you can see, these varieties open like garden roses. Roses always look more spectacular when they are open, so try to allow them a long time to condition before arranging them as they will then fill out an arrangement better. If you only need the flowers for one night, then it is best to use them fully open. If you wish to enjoy the arrangement for a longer period, you should choose your flowers carefully for their long-lasting qualities.

4 Add the grapes and fill any gaps in the arrangement with foliage.

Add the sweet peas last because they are the most delicate and fragile of all the flowers used here (*right*). Mist the flowers and floral foam frequently to prolong the life of the arrangement.

Anthurium flowers consist of a shiny, waxy bract called a spathe, with a central protruding cylindrical spadix (spike-like cluster of flowers). They bruise easily and, because they look so unusual and have an almost artificial, plastic-like quality, it is common for people to pinch them to see if they are real. Unfortunately, this leaves a mark. The flowers are also affected by the salt which is carried on the surface of human skin, so try to avoid touching the spathes.

The name "anthurium" comes from the Greek – *anthos* means flowers and *oura* means tail, which refers to the spadix. Both the spathes and the spadices grow in many different colours and shadings. Some varieties look deformed and are useful for creative and abstract arrangements. Others are suitable for ikebana (Japanese flower arranging).

Anthuriums are very easy to condition and should last for anything from ten days to three weeks in the correct surroundings. When you receive the flowers, remove the water phial, cut off at least 1 inch (2.5 cm) of the stem at an angle with a pair of sharp scissors and place in fresh water containing flower-food. Like all tropical flowers, anthuriums prefer a high level of humidity, do not like dry, air-conditioned environments, and should be kept in constant conditions out of draughts. If the temperature falls below 41° F (5° C) or the flowers are exposed to draughts, the petals will soon turn black or become limp. As they do not take up much water when they are cut, the flowers benefit from frequent misting with water to increase their humidity levels. If an anthurium flower does start to become limp, you may be able to revive it by submerging it in warm water for approximately 15 minutes.

A. 'Tropical' is the most common red variety. I like the variegated forms such as 'Greenpeace', which is green and white with a pink spadix, and the cream and pale pink 'Fantasia', which takes its name from Walt Disney's pink elephants and has such a perfect line around the bract that it looks as though someone has drawn it. 'Surprise' has very similar colourings and markings. My favourite varieties are the green 'Midori' and 'Cuba', both of which can be softened and used with flowing foliage, such as eucalyptus (*Eucalyptus*). The green and white varieties can be used as a backdrop to purple lilac (*Syringa*) and roses (*Rosa*). The red anthuriums are useful at Christmas and for Valentine's Day, and I like the heart-shaped, deep red 'Honduras' variety when combined with the red Singapore orchid (*Dendrobium* 'James Storei') and green cymbidium (*Cymbidium*) orchids with dark red noses. These are framed with twisted, dried clematis (*Clematis*) vine, fashioned into a heart shape, to make a long-lasting and unusual alternative to red roses.

Left: Miniature anthuriums have been grouped together with *Begonia* leaves and *Crocosmia* seed heads on a contemporary metal pedestal.
Above right: Several 'Tropical' anthuriums have been arranged in a posy so that the spathes look like petals.

ANTHURIUMS IN A PUMPKIN

MATERIALS

Large pumpkin (*Curcubita maxima*)

Knife and pair of sharp scissors

Sheet of plastic

Floral foam

Oak leaves (*Quercus*)

Rose hips (*Rosa canina*)

Hypericum 'Autumn Blaze' berries

Ornamental chili peppers (*Capsicum*)

Bulrushes (*Typha latifolia*)

Nerines (*Nerine sarniensis*

 'Corsica Major')

Trusses of tomatoes (*Lycopersicum*)

Heavy florist's wire

'Scarletta' anthuriums (*Anthurium*)

1 This arrangement is intended for a special occasion. To start it, choose a well-balanced pumpkin with a flat base. Slice off the top of the pumpkin and cut out a large hole in the flesh without piercing the skin. Line the pumpkin with a sheet of thick plastic. Soak the floral foam in water, then cut it to fit in the hole snugly, making sure that it sits higher than the pumpkin rim so you will be able to arrange foliage and flowers in a cascade down the sides to soften the arrangement.

2 Establish the basic shape of the arrangement with sprigs of oak leaves. The height of the foliage should be twice that of the container – this is a general rule for all flower arranging. Add trails of rose hips randomly through the leaves and fill any other gaps with the hypericum berries.

3 Arrange the branches of ornamental chili peppers (you can buy these as cut flowers) by pushing their stems into the floral foam. Place the bulrushes throughout the arrangement to add height and arrange the nerines through the foliage to establish the overall shape. The trusses of tomatoes can be wired in place with heavy florist's wire twisted around their stems. Check that all the floral foam is covered.

Now begin to add the focal flowers – the 'Scarletta' anthuriums (*right*). These are very dominating so leave plenty of space around each flower and check that all the spadices point outward. Each spadix is slightly different, so think carefully about its appearance before arranging it. Keep the finished arrangement in a cool place and periodically top up the floral foam with water. If you cannot obtain a suitable pumpkin, you can use other squashes or a large watermelon.

I A S

Above: Spiky *Heliconia caribaea* 'Lamark' cv. 'Kawauchi' and hanging *H. rostrata* 'Ruiz and Pavon' are used in a vase bound by stag's-horn fern (*Platycerium*

bifurcatum). This fern is an epiphytic plant – it grows on other plants without being a parasite – which I purchased mounted on a piece of board.

Above: The elegance of these thin heliconias (*H. psittacorum* 'Helena'), is mirrored by the yucca (*Yucca*) tips arranged around the vase with double-sided adhesive tape (*see page* 84). This variety of heliconia also grows in pink, yellow, red and two-tone colours.

HELICONIAS IN A DECORATED VASE

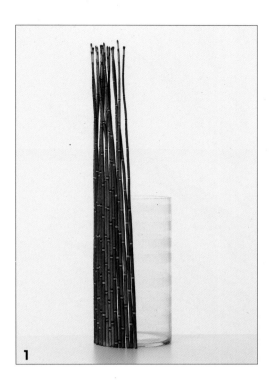

MATERIALS

Double-sided adhesive tape

Cylindrical glass vase

Bundle of snake grass

(*Scirpus tabernaemontani* 'Zebrinus')

Scissors and knife

Bundle of raffia

Dogwood (*Cornus*) twigs

Heliconias (*Heliconia bihai*

'Emerald Forest' and 'Nappi')

Yucca (*Yucca aloifolia*) leaves

New Zealand flax (*Phormium*) leaves

1 Apply several strips of double-sided adhesive tape to the outer surface of the glass vase, from top to bottom. Continue sticking this around the vase until it is completely covered. Stick a single strand of snake grass at a time to the vase, working from bottom to top. Be selective when choosing the snake grass as some strands are straighter than others, and these are the ones you need to use. Snake grass grows in swampy, tropical areas and has been highly cultivated in Florida. Other reeds, such as mikado grass, would give the same effect as snake grass, or you could use yucca tips, as shown in the photograph on page 83.

2 Continue until the whole vase has been covered. Cut the raffia into no less than 12 strips at least double the circumference of the vase. Tie all the raffia around the vase, knot it tightly and trim the ends. The snake grass will dry out and last indefinitely, but its colour will fade in time.

3 Carefully trim the top of the snake grass so it is flush with the top of the glass vase. Fill the vase with tepid water, then add some flower-food.

Arrange the dogwood twigs in the vase first, as they will help to anchor the large heliconias (*right*). Trim the heliconias to length and arrange them in the vase. Finally, add the yucca and flax leaves, which give extra colour and interest to the arrangement.

H E L I C O N

Right: One of the most widely available types of heliconia (*Heliconia*) is the erect *H. caribaea* 'Vermilion Lake'.

Above, from left to right: This pendant variety of *H. rostrata* 'Ruiz and Pavon' is more commonly referred

to as a hanging heliconia and is useful for large, dramatic arrangements; this delicate variety of

H. latispatha 'Gyro' is just one of an enormous range available throughout the year.

These flowers are natives of the American tropics and are principally grown in Central Mexico, South

America and the Caribbean. They are now cultivated on the Ivory Coast of Africa, in Kenya, South Africa,

Australia and Israel, as well as in hothouses in other flower-producing areas of the world. In parts of Europe

such as Britain and France, which historically have had links with the West Indies, an excellent supply of

heliconias (*Heliconia*) is available thanks to direct air transport. The flowers are imported into the United

States from the West Indies – including Jamaica, Trinidad and Tobago – and from Costa Rica. Heliconias are

usually available throughout the year, although each species has its own particular season.

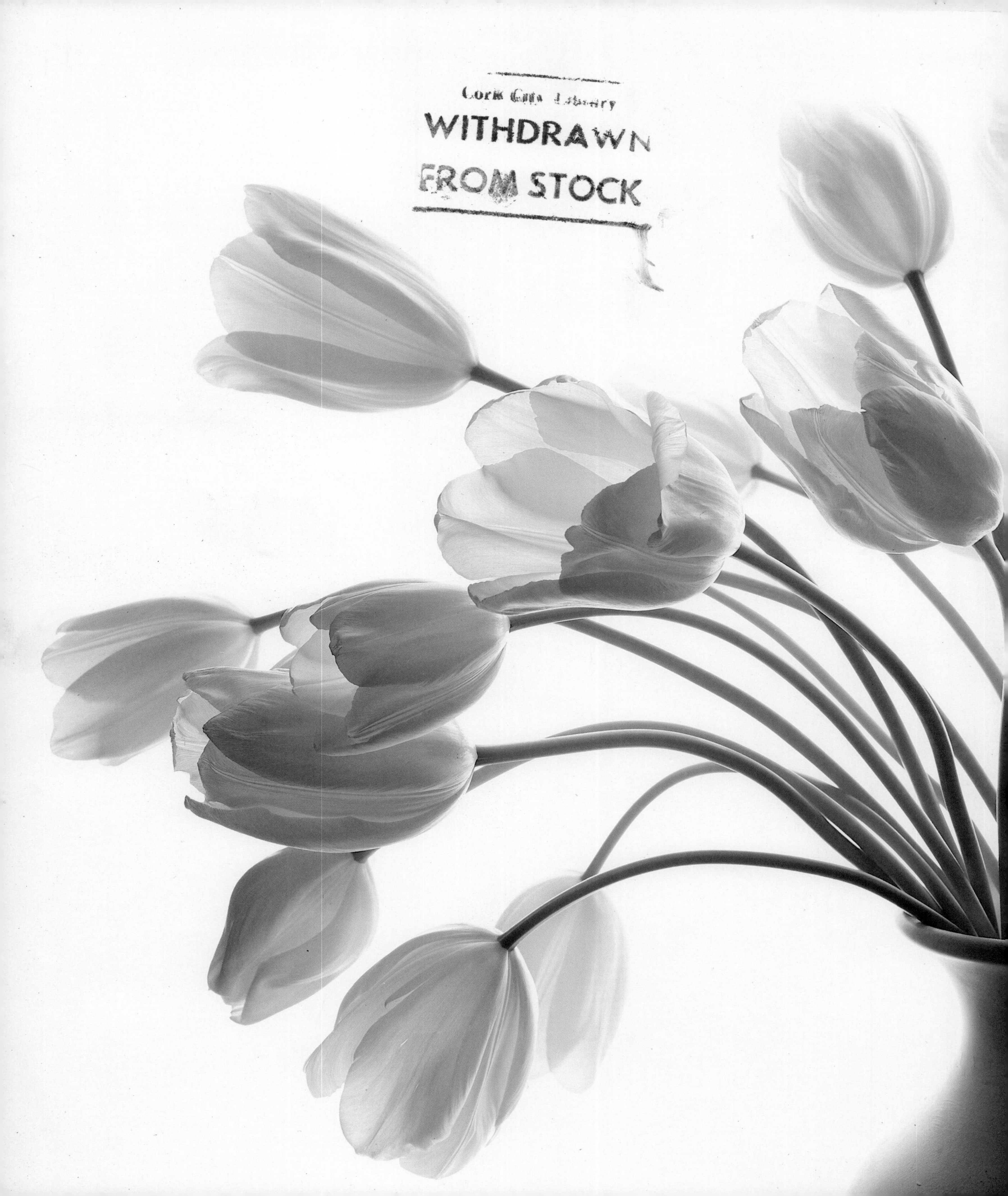

Each day, about 350 different colours and shades of gerbera are sold at the Dutch flower auctions. Popular colours are grown in other flower-producing regions of the world too, notably Israel. These hybrids are now in the top ten of the best-selling flowers in the world. Gerberas are harvested and grouped according to their colour. They are then post-harvest treated – left for several hours in a solution known as a pulse treatment which injects strength into the flowers for their onward journey and keeps the stems erect until they reach the retailer. Huge baths are filled with this solution so that many flowers can be treated at the same time.

arrangements. If you purchase half or a whole box of them, condition them upright with the flowerheads erect. The best way to do this is to stand them in a full bucket of water. After conditioning them, it is a good idea to add a little household bleach to their flower water as they are susceptible to bacterial attack. Add one quarter of a teaspoon (1.5 ml) of household bleach to 1 gallon (4.5 litres) of warm water.

Gerbera stems are leafless but very hairy, and can turn mushy and weak if left in deep water for too long. For this reason, you should condition them in deep water but arrange them in not more than 2–3 inches (5–7.5 cm) of

Ideally, gerberas should always be conditioned in water that is just tepid and to which a special gerbera food has been added. If the flowers are limp on arrival, cut at least 1 inch (2.5 cm) off the stems at an angle, then carefully wrap the stems in newspaper without damaging the flowerheads and place them in tepid water and flower-food. If you do not support the stems they will harden up into whichever position they are in, which may be an impossible shape for flower

water. The stems vary considerably in length and some are quite short, owing to the nature of their packing. I wish some growers would develop packaging for extra-tall gerberas. When I use gerberas in large arrangements – and they are very useful for providing focal points and colour – I often have to use flower extension cones, which are funnels filled with water and supported on garden canes, into which the flowers are placed. These cones are available from florists.

Left: Smaller gerberas are known as mini gerberas or, affectionately, as germinis. Here, 'Paso' gerberas are mixed with aspidistra (*Aspidistra*) leaves. In the base of the arrangement, matching orange tulips (*Tulipa*) are encircled by South African reeds set in an ornamental terracotta flowerpot.

Above: This idea was inspired by a Tex-Mex party. The orange 'Paso', yellow 'Polka' and red 'Salsa' germinis are wired onto a large cactus.

TRAILING ARRANGEMENT WITH GERBERAS

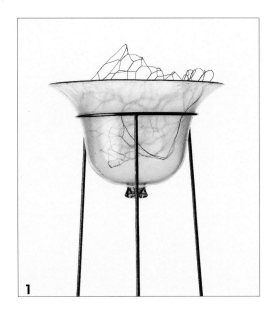

MATERIALS

Glass bowl on a stand

2-inch (5-cm) gauge wire mesh

Virginia creeper (*Vitis quinquefolia*)

Eucalyptus (*Eucalyptus*) pods

Liguster privet (*Ligustrum*) berries

Trailing ivy (*Hedera*)

Guelder rose (*Viburnum opulus*) berries

Assorted autumnal or fall foliage

Hypericum (*Hypericum*) berries

Crocosmia seed heads

Old man's beard (*Clematis vitalba*)

Leucospermum leutens

Love-lies-bleeding (*Amaranthus*)

Yellow 'Tamara', orange 'Barcelona'

and red 'Bordeaux' gerberas (*Gerbera*)

1 Fill the container with fresh water mixed with flower-food, then add some 2-inch (5-cm) gauge wire mesh. Scrunch it up to fit the bowl snugly.

2 Begin by arranging the foliage in the shape of the finished arrangement. Choose good, trailing foliage to complement the stand and fuller, bushier foliage for the upright placings.

3 A natural-looking arrangement like this requires a variety of foliage, with berries and pods providing interest and texture. Seed heads add rich colour too, and in this arrangement I have used *Crocosmia* seed heads and old man's beard, which I especially like because I saw it growing in the Suffolk hedgerows when I was a child. For conservation reasons, you should never gather flowers from the wild, so

it is a good idea to grow your own wild plants for arranging. In the United Kingdom, a wide range of foliage can be bought from florists because there is a tradition of arranging flowers with deciduous foliage and large estates still supply foliage to the country's main flower markets. Add the *Leucospermum leutens* and the trailing plumes of the love-lies-bleeding to the arrangement.

Add the gerberas in groups of three to avoid the arrangement looking patchy and to make it rich, bold and dramatic (*right*). I have chosen foliage and flowers that are very complementary. The colours of this arrangement make it suitable for a harvest or Thanksgiving supper. Mist the foliage regularly and make sure you keep the container topped up with water.

S U N F L O W

Above, from left to right: *Helianthus annus* 'Teddy Bear'; *H.a.* 'Taiyo'; *H.a.* 'Avondzon'; *H.a.* 'Primrose'.

Right: A flowerhead of *H.* Chrysanthemum-flowered series.

Sunflowers have become the vogue flowers of the 1990s. They are universally loved for their happy, smiling

faces and they make popular gifts for men because of their strong and masculine appearance. Their name,

Helianthus, comes from the Greek – *helios* means sun and *anthos* means flower. At one time, the sunflower was

seasonal but now, because of its widespread cultivation, particularly in Israel, it is available almost every

week of the year from some sunny climate or other. There are about 150 different species of herbaceous

annual and perennial sunflowers throughout the world, although they appear mostly in the Americas where

they have been adapted to a wide range of climates, including wetlands, arid grasslands and rich fertile soil,

as well as roadsides and wastelands. Where humans have gone, sunflowers have followed because of the food

value of their seeds which are an important source of vegetable oil.

sunflowers

Right: Sunflowers are perfect for large, spectacular displays. *Helianthus annus* 'Taiyo' is mixed with *Eremurus, Celosia, Hedychium gardnerianum* and the seed heads of the lotus flower (*Nelumbo nucifera*). The arrangement is flanked by huge tropical elephant's ears (*Colocasia esculenta*) and cut stalks to add architectural interest.

Above, from left to right: *Paeonia* 'Duchesse de Nemours'; *P*. 'Avant Garde'; *P*. 'Auguste Dessert'.

Right: About 30 varieties of peony are cultivated for the cut flower trade. The fluffy double

P. 'Sarah Bernhardt' is the most popular peony sold as a cut flower.

PEONIES

Peonies belong to the Ranunculaceae family, which is one of the most handsome in the plant kingdom. These

sensational and showy flowers are universally popular and their relationship with mankind can be traced

back through history and into mythology. The genus name of *Paeonia* comes from Panon the Doctor, who was

a Greek god. Some species, indeed, are known to have medicinal qualities. By far the commonest group of

peonies are the pink varieties, which include the extremely popular and versatile

'Sarah Bernhardt', yet few people are aware of how many different shades are available,

ranging from the deepest crimson through to pale peach and a soft yellow. Some peonies are also

scented, such as the richly perfumed 'Duchesse de Nemours' and 'White Wings', both of which are white.

Peonies can be divided into two main types: herbaceous (which die down in autumn or fall) and tree peonies (which do not). Tree peonies do not travel as well as their herbaceous cousins and the flowers do not last as long when cut. Both types produce a variety of flowerheads: single; double; anemone-form which resemble anemones; and the bomb varieties which are so called because they are round.

From their birthplace in China, where they symbolize spring, peonies were first introduced to Europe in the sixteenth century, when they were planted in knot gardens with such timeless classics as lavender (*Lavandula*), jasmine (*Jasminum*), lilies (*Lilium*) and rosemary (*Rosmarinus*). Although peonies are often considered to be quintessentially English flowers, it is the French who were responsible for their development. This is why so many varieties have romantic French names, such as 'Souvenir de Maxime Cornu', 'Auguste Dessert', 'Felix Crousse' and 'Duchesse de Nemours'.

One of the principal reasons that peonies are so popular is that they last well as cut flowers if harvested while still in bud. In Japan, where they are second only to chrysanthemums (*Chrysanthemum*) in popularity, they are known as the plant of twenty days, because that is the anticipated time for the flowers to bloom and remain fresh. While this may be an over-estimation of their life as a cut flower, peonies will still provide good service if they are conditioned well.

Left: A mixture of lady's mantle (*Alchemilla mollis*) with the peonies 'Sarah Bernhardt', 'Duchesse de Nemours', 'Karl Rosenfeld', 'Shirley Temple' and 'China Rose' which has a yellow, anemone-like centre.

When found growing in their natural habitat, the most conspicuous varieties of heliconia live in moist sites along roadways, riverbanks and in patches of open ground in tropical rainforests. Hummingbirds and bats are attracted to the pink, orange, red and yellow colours of the flowers and bracts, and so act as pollinators. In the past, heliconias have been variously associated with the banana, strelitzia and ginger families, to which they are closely related, but they have their own family of Heliconiaceae. Heliconias are cut when the crop is fully grown and the flowers mature. The flowers are either erect or pendant (hanging) and are usually red, yellow or orange, or combinations of these colours, sometimes in zigzag patterns. They have no scent, but their striking appearance more than makes up for this. There are some green varieties, and these are among my favourites. Most heliconia flowers are smooth and fleshy, but some are covered in woolly hairs, such as the red *H. vellerigera* from South Africa which has cinnamon hairs. *H. danielsiana* 'Kress' is brown and hairy, and grows in Florida. The leaves, stalks and even the fruits are all useful and fun to use in flower arranging.

Generally, heliconias are air-freighted to their destination. As they are very heavy, every box of heliconias has a very high air-freight value and, consequently, the cost per stem is high. I take real pleasure in opening a box of heliconias which have come straight from the Windward Islands, because the brightly coloured specimens arrive carefully wrapped in local newspapers, with handwritten instructions on how to condition the flowers.

To condition heliconias, use a pair of sharp scissors to cut off the bottom inch (2.5 cm) of stem, plus any superfluous leaves and stalks, and place in tepid water to which a sachet of flower-food has been added. Heliconias need to be kept in a room free from draughts and above 41° F (5° C), otherwise they will prematurely age. For this reason, they are often sold wrapped in plastic to keep them warm. They are not suited to being stored in commercial cooling units and prefer a humid environment, so beware of buying them from stalls where they have been kept out of water or in the cold, open air. Healthy specimens have a good colour and their petals show no signs of curling up and turning black, both of which are signs that the flowers are past their prime.

Above: Sturdy, robust containers, like the one used here, are necessary to support the thick and heavy stems of heliconias to avoid them over-balancing. Papyrus (*Cyperus papyrus*), screw pine (*Pendanus*) and *Curculigo* give an interesting, contemporary shape to what is a simple arrangement.

Right: A colourful tropical tree can be created with lengths of freshly cut bamboo bound together to make a stalk, with a large ball of floral foam impaled on top. I used a hanging heliconia (*H. chartacea* 'Sexy Pink'), Queen palm (*Arecastrum*) and palm leaves (*Phoenix roebelini*), gingers (*Alpinia purpurata*), (*Costus pulverulentus*), rattlers (*Calathea crotalifera*) and anthuriums (*Anthurium*) 'Greenpeace'.

G

Left: Over 500 varieties of gerbera are sold each year in the Dutch auctions and new varieties are tested each week. It is therefore difficult to identify specific varieties and only the very popular ones have been labelled in this chapter.

Above, from left to right: The yellow 'Geel Zwago', although a better way to order this would be to say "yellow with a black eye"; the tangerine semi-double 'King'; the red 'Roulette'; and a new shaggy variety called 'Doctor Who'.

E R B E R A S

Who can resist the charm and innocence of these happy flowers? They look almost too perfect to be real. In 1937, Vita Sackville-West included the gerbera as one of her favourite flowers in her small book, *Some Flowers*. She had first spotted one in a florist's but was unable to discover the name of this bright, neat flower. Later, she found it again at a flower show and discovered that it was called the Transvaal daisy, or *Gerbera jamesonii*. "Neither name pleased me very much, but the flower itself pleased me very much indeed. It seemed to include every colour one could most desire", she wrote. No other cut flower offers the range of colours which gerberas can provide. In addition to single-coloured, there are double-coloured and the new fringed gerberas. Some gerberas have black eyes and others have green centres. They have no scent and are sold without foliage, but they can be bought as a houseplant which lasts for about three weeks.

gerberas

Right: These are some very popular colours, displayed simply in different-coloured glass bow vases. From left to right: dark red 'Bordeaux'; yellow 'Tamara'; deep burgundy 'Chateau'; bright orange 'Tennessee'; cerise-pink 'Fredigor'; and yellow 'Dallas'.

SUNFLOWER BALL WITH PEPPERS

MATERIALS

About 25 sunflowers

(*Helianthus annus* 'Taiyo')

Knife

Length of rope or sea grass

Pair of sharp scissors

Tall cylindrical glass vase

About 20 red and yellow peppers

(*Capsicum*)

3 bromeliad (*Neoregelia carolinae*

'Meyendorfii') rosettes

1 Take a few sunflowers and strip the stems clean of all foliage. Create the rounded top of a circle by bunching the stems together in your hand with the flowerheads facing outward. Hold the flowers very high on the stem. Choose flowerheads as uniform in size as possible to create an arrangement that looks balanced.

2 Once you are happy with the shape, tie the base of the heads together with a length of rope or sea grass, as I have used here. Continue to arrange the flowerheads in a circle, always binding in the new ones when you are happy with their placement, until you have created a well-rounded ball of sunflower heads. It might look slightly irregular but do not worry as this adds

to the charm, and the impact of the overall arrangement takes the eye away from any imperfections.

3 When you have completed the ball of flowerheads, trim all the stems with a pair of sharp scissors so they stand upright. Tie the stems together about three-quarters of the way down with rope or sea grass. Place in the middle of a heavy, cylindrical glass vase. While still holding the sunflower ball in the middle of the vase, begin to arrange the peppers around the base of the stems.

4 Continue to add the peppers, taking care to build up a patchwork effect by arranging a random mix of yellow and red. I have chosen to use peppers because of their glossy, colourful skins

and pleasing shapes, and also because they last well in water. Alternatively, you could use small chili peppers, small red onions, citrus fruits or something seasonal and inexpensive, but whatever you choose, it must be a fruit or vegetable that will survive being submerged in water without decaying.

When you are happy with the arrangement, check it from all angles, then fill the vase with cold water (*right*). Cut off any pieces of string that are dangling down. To soften the rim of the vase and complete the base, add some bromeliad rosettes which are sold as a cut flower. As an alternative, you can use the leaves of a bromeliad houseplant, but remove all traces of soil before adding them to the water.

Above: A linear arrangement of different varieties of sunflowers combined with 'Arabian Night' dahlias (*Dahlia*) for the top layer. The base of the

arrangement consists of tansies (*Tanacetum*), chocolate cosmos (*Cosmos atrosanguineus*), white dill (*Anethum*) and blackberry stems (*Rubus fruiticosus*).

Right: Smaller varieties of sunflowers are excellent for arranging in posies with summer flowers such as *Hypericum*, green dill (*Anethum*),

Rudbeckia, *Zinnia*, *Dicentra spectabilis*, *Helenium* and wheat ears (*Triticum*), hops (*Humulus*) and *Leucadendron* 'Safari Sunset' as foliage.

The thrill of discovering sunflowers growing wild on hillsides and grass verges while I was driving through the United States usually meant that my journeys would be delayed while I stopped and marvelled at them. To me, it is very appropriate that the sunflower should be the national flower of the United States because it shares some of its characteristics with the country and it originated here. I think it is the perfect American plant – bold, optimistic, tenacious, mighty, powerful and sassy. A rather more important reason for the sunflower being the quintessential American flower is that it is the only one of world economic importance to originate in the United States.

In southern Spain, Italy and France, where they are grown for their seeds, sunflowers are breathtaking to behold en masse. It is humbling, yet exhilarating at the same time, to walk through a field of sunflowers and examine the obedient way in which they follow the sun's path with their heads, like ranks of well-drilled soldiers. Before dawn, the flower-heads will still be facing west from the previous evening's sunset but, as the sun rises, they will soon swing from the west to the east to welcome the sun's early morning rays. This movement is repeated each day until pollination is complete, the ovaries contained in the flowerhead are fertilized and the flowerhead is heavy with its developing seeds. The heavy flowerhead then bows down, pregnant with its crop.

Sunflowers are tremendously colourful, and their glorious frill of yellow petals attract insects for pollination. They have had a long domestic association. Carbon-dating suggests the existence of sunflowers growing at least 1500 years ago in Colombia, South America, and this country is one of the biggest exporters of these cheerful flowers.

The face of a sunflower consists of an outer frill of daisy-like petals and a centre crammed with seeds arranged in a dense, honeycomb pattern. The flowers are typically yellow, with a green, brown or near-black centre, although brown and maroon varieties are becoming increasingly available. The double forms have fluffy, yellow petals. There are both annual and perennial varieties of sunflower, but the giant-headed annual blooms are better-loved than the smaller, perennial flowers. The flowers vary considerably in size and range from large heads that are as much as 6 inches (15 cm) across to smaller ones about 1 inch (2.5 cm) in diameter. Equally, you can choose between dwarf varieties, which grow to no more than 2 feet (60 cm), or tall annuals, which will tower over you at 10 feet (3.3 metres) or more. The most popular varieties are the perennial semi-double *Helianthus decapetalus* 'Soleil d'Or', and the single and double forms of *H. annus*. The perennial *H. decapetalus* 'Loddon Gold' has only a limited season, but its double flowers last for a long time in water.

When the shaggy flowers arrive in my shop after a long-haul flight they sometimes look ready to be discarded. My staff have often unpacked sunflowers and complained that they look half-dead, only to find the following day that they have revived and turned into an army of cheerful, erect and alert smiling faces. Once cut, these flowers need plenty of water, so I would advise that you transport them in water whenever possible. It is hard to generalize about how long they will last as cut flowers, but one or two weeks is a realistic time span. When you condition the sunflowers, use a pair of sharp scissors to cut off at least 1 inch (2.5 cm) at the base of the stem in a slanting cut, remove all the foliage to lengthen the life of the cut flowers, then put them in plenty of fresh water into which you have dissolved some flower-food.

The brown centres of the large varieties, which are grown for their seeds, are occasionally cut and auctioned at the Dutch flower auctions, and then exported. These huge, ripe seed heads can measure almost 12 inches (30 cm) in diameter and provide texture and an element of surprise in flower arrangements. When we have had large quantities of sunflowers which have become damaged in the shop, I have stripped them of their petals and used the seed heads as foliage for tied bunches or to give added interest and texture to larger arrangements. Used on their own, the seed heads look very good if they are fixed, with a hot glue gun, to the outside of a container. This works very well when a mixture of brown, black and yellow seed heads is used because the diversity in texture and colour looks like patchwork.

Right: It is fun to take your inspiration for flower arrangements from some of the Old Masters, and Van Gogh's *Sunflowers* was my starting point here. I mixed sunflowers with *Banksia*, pineapple lilies (*Eucomis*), bronze chrysanthemums (*Chrysanthemum* 'Tom Pearce'), red robin (*Photina*) foliage, proteas (*Protea repens*), bear grass (*Dasylirion*) and zebra grass (*Miscanthus sinensis* 'Zebrinus').

Above: 'Sarah Bernhardt', 'Shirley Temple', 'China Rose' and 'Knighthood' peonies in a heart-shaped basket.

Right: Waterlilies (*Nymphaea* 'Attraction') are floated around a single 'Sarah Bernhardt' peony.

When buying peonies, choose those that are just opening, with buds that show colour and feel soft to the touch. Peony buds that are as hard as bullets are unripe and will rarely open. Condition the flowers by cutting at least 1 inch (2.5 cm) off the bottom of the stems at a slanting angle with a pair of sharp scissors. Then place in water into which some flower-food has been dissolved. It is always advisable to buy your peonies between late April and June, when they are in season. As it is possible to keep herbaceous peonies in a cool place without water for up to seven days, they make good world travellers and it is not uncommon to see peonies in the United Kingdom which have been flown in from as far away as Australia and New Zealand. It is also possible to find Dutch peonies all over the world, even in sun-drenched California, so do ask your supplier about the country of origin if you are in doubt. Peonies last well in cold storage, which means that some of them are kept in this way at the end of each season. Such flowers will never last as long as those sold in season, and should only be used when it is absolutely necessary to do so.

One way to combat the problem of the peony's short season is to use the flowers dried. Peonies can be dried by air or by desiccant, and large commercial companies have recently been experimenting with freeze-drying methods, with breathtakingly realistic results. Well-known varieties, such as 'Sarah Bernhardt', are often dried, although all peonies can be dried with care.

The large heads of peonies make them very suitable for basing, which is the floristry term for using flowerheads cut short and arranged very close together. Basing is often employed for sculptural designs or for creating such images as names, logos and badges, and it has become a feature of sympathy floral design in the United Kingdom. The skill of basing lies in being able to mass the flowers together while still retaining the shape of the design, such as a heart. Usually, based arrangements have a bevelled effect, which gives a rounded shape from the base to the middle and back again. Peonies are ideal for this because they give maximum coverage and their fluffy petals overlap to hide the floral foam. The heart arrangement (*facing page*) shows the faces of the flowers.

111

BASKET OF PEONIES

MATERIALS

Floral foam and floral foam tape

Twig basket

Sheets of plastic

Sprigs of oak (*Quercus*) leaves

Variegated ivy (*Hedera*) trails

Spirea (*Spirea*)

Spurge (*Euphorbia polychroma*)

Firethorn (*Pyracantha*)

Millet grass (*Milium*)

Green dill (*Anethum graveolens*)

Achillea (*Achillea filipendulina*)

Nigella damascena seed heads

Yellow cornflowers (*Centaurea dealbata*)

Marguerite daisies

  (*Chrysanthemum frutescens*)

'Duchesse de Nemours' peonies (*Paeonia*)

1 branch of crab apples (*Malus*)

1 This is a classic English basket arrangement which florists call single-ended because the stems of the flowers are visible at one end to give a natural, "just-picked" look. The same principle can be used without the basket, when the arrangement is known as a single-ended spray. Start by soaking a block of floral foam in water until it is thoroughly wet. Line the basket with the plastic, add the foam and secure it in position with floral foam tape.

2 Arrange the sprigs of oak leaves around the edge of the basket and through the handle, to give the desired shape. Cut off smaller sprigs of oak leaves and place them as deep in the floral foam as possible so the leaves can continue to take up water.

3 Choose a good range of flowering foliage to provide interest and texture. Variegated ivy softens the edges of the basket arrangement and the flowering spirea and spurge create different textures. Continue cutting small sprigs of foliage to cover the floral foam in the top end of the basket.

4 Trim the flowers, but save all the stalks so you can add them later. Place the larger-headed achillea as deep into the foliage as possible and position the *Nigella* and cornflower heads higher in the arrangement. When placing the marguerites, do not let them dominate the arrangement.

Add the open peony heads and fill in any spaces with crab apples or peony buds (*right*). If you wish, you can hide the basket's handle, as I have done. Arrange the flower stalks, which you saved earlier, in the floral foam at the bottom end of the basket. Fill in between them with more foliage and twine ivy trails through the stalks.

3

4

Above: Peonies can be used in innovative ways by mixing them with tropical flowers and creating a clashing colour effect. Here they are used with *Achillea*, 'Nicole' roses, *Celosia* and arum lilies (*Zantedeschia rehmannii*).

The ruff of *Anthurium* leaves is trimmed with lotus (*Nelumbo*) flowers.

Right: I made a raft from South African reeds tied with sea grass. I then wired a spray tray filled with floral foam into the middle, and arranged a mixture of sea holly (*Eryngium maritimum*), chincherinchees (*Ornithogalum*), poppy (*Papaver*) seed heads, white 'Duchesse de Nemours' peonies, bells of Ireland (*Moluccella laevis*) and arum lilies (*Zantedeschia aethiopica*).

Peonies can also be used in a more dramatic way, combining them with hot-coloured exotic flowers such as cock's comb (*Celosia*), painter's palette (*Anthurium*) leaves and waterlilies (*Nymphaea*). This creates a more modern style and uses the texture and colours of the flowers to the full. You can also use peonies in a minimal fashion, as I have done in the raft arrangement (*right*). Arrangements of this sort make excellent centre pieces, especially if you use a combination of familiar and more unusual flowers and foliage, because they provide a focal point and can be studied at close-quarters.

In its native China, the red peony was considered to be the king of flowers because of its rich colour and bulbous shape. As a result, it became a symbol of abundance. By contrast, in nineteenth-century Britain and the United States, the flower was given the meaning of bashfulness, and so it became popular for weddings. It is available from May to July each year, at the height of the wedding season, which makes it a perfect flower for posies, bridal bouquets and head-dresses. The illustration on page 117 shows how a simple, summery bouquet can be made by tying flowers together. Peonies are easy to wire, last well, and can be manipulated into many forms. I often use the wired heads with bay (*Laurus*) leaves and sprigs of rosemary (*Rosmarinus*) to line the rim and the interior of a serving basket. A selection of wired peonies also makes a spectacular yet charming garland for a flower girl or bridesmaid to hold.

Peonies are still seasonal flowers, which is part of their charm. Although I could sell them for 52 weeks of the year in my shop, I am grateful that they are not always available because their rarity adds to their immense beauty and style. Some things are best left seasonal and I would never want these flowers to become an all-year staple and lose their attraction as fragrant seasonal favourites. At one time, peonies were known as "the poor man's rose", but now they are considerably more valuable than that commercial flower which is always in season.

Above: Peonies are the classic wedding flower. They are shown here in a tied bouquet with scented honeysuckle (*Lonicera*) trails, love-lies-bleeding (*Amaranthus*), arum lilies (*Zantedeschia rehmannii*), 'Nicole' roses (*Rosa*), mock orange (*Philadelphus*) and borage (*Borago*). It is helpful when arranging a bouquet like this to do it looking in a mirror so you can see how the shape is developing and make sure that all the flowers are facing forward.

Left: A woodland display of copper beech (*Fagus*) leaves, peonies and foxgloves (*Digitalis*), with marsh dock (*Rumex palustris*) and euphorbia (*Euphorbia fulgens*), which has cascades of tiny white florets on droopy stems and is very useful for softening the look of an arrangement.

A M

Left: 'Telstar' is one of the strongest and largest amaryllis.

Above, from left to right: The red and white 'Minerva'; the best-known white cultivar,

'Ludwig Dazzler'; 'Red Lion' is the most popular amaryllis of all, and is in

especial demand each Christmas because of its colour.

A R Y L L I S

The name "amaryllis" is confusing, because traditionally it refers to *Amaryllis belladonna*, which is the true

amaryllis, and not to the flowers in this chapter, which are *Hippeastrum* hybrids. However, it is these

Hippeastrum hybrids which have been developed extensively and are widely referred to across the world as

amaryllis, in both cut flower and bulb forms. Botanists originally grouped these flowers together, but they

are now classed separately. The hybrid *Hippeastrum* flowers are available from September to May, with their

peak season at Christmas. *A. belladonna* is aptly named for its dazzling beauty, as the flowers are certainly

impressive when they are in full bloom. They are only available in August and September.

In this chapter, I am using *Hippeastrum* flowers but have given them their common name of amaryllis. These giant flowers are raised from bulbs and produce a hollow stem crowned with anything from two to five flowerheads. Occasionally, a bulb will produce more than one stem. Amaryllis are rare and expensive when bought as cut flowers, and they are more usually raised from the bulbs which are often sold at Christmas in a decorative box. They make popular and attractive gifts for their green-fingered recipients.

Whether you buy them as cut flowers or raise your amaryllis yourself, you will find that the stems can grow perilously tall and, when cut, may have to be internally supported by being plugged with a sturdy stick. The traditional remedy is to plug the stems with water and cotton wool, but I find this very time-consuming and not altogether successful, especially for the longevity of the cut flower. I find it much easier to use a simple bamboo or green garden cane. These are inconspicuous and can be trimmed

Above: 'Red Velvet' amaryllis, holly (*Ilex*) and larch (*Larix*) leaves. The nightlights are covered in laurel (*Laurelia*) leaves.
Right: This topiary tree shape is made by arranging a group of 'Telstar' amaryllis neatly together and binding them just beneath their flowerheads. They are kept upright in the dish with a flower arranger's pin cushion, concealed by pebbles.

to the desired length with a pair of secateurs after they have been inserted in the flower stems. If you do not have any suitable canes you can use twigs, flexible willow (*Salix*) wands or hard stems from other flowers such as *Strelitzia*.

Amaryllis can be used in floral foam, but they will need to be carefully conditioned first. Cut no less than 1 inch (2.5 cm) off the bottom of the stem at an angle, and leave for several hours in a solution of water and flower-food. These flowers also need careful placing – ideally, you should use wire mesh rather than floral foam to support them, as this will let them drink freely through their hollow stems. While in water, the flower retains considerable amounts of liquid within the stem, so take care when removing the flower from water as the residue in the stem will drain out and could spill over delicate surfaces. After several weeks the stems may split, but if you recut them above the split the flowers will continue to perform, although your arrangement will be shorter. Give the flowers fresh water and flower-food at regular intervals.

FESTIVE ARRANGEMENT WITH AMARYLLIS

1

2

3

MATERIALS

Floral foam fix and floral foam tape

Florist's "frog"

Fruit bowl on a pedestal

Soaked floral foam

Heavy florist's wire

1 large church candle

Variegated holly (*Ilex*)

Ivy (*Hedera*) berries

Skimmia japonica berries

Ornamental chili peppers (*Capsicum*)

Rambutans

Tamarillos

Larch (*Larix*) twigs

'Minerva' amaryllis (*Hippeastrum*)

1 Using some floral foam fix, place a "frog" in the base of the fruit bowl to secure the soaked floral foam. "Frogs" are available from florists. Make four hairpins or bobby pins from the heavy florist's wire and tape them onto the bottom of the candle to enable you to anchor it in the floral foam.

2 Position the floral foam to stand above the edge of the container. This allows you to place the foliage horizontally and therefore soften the look of the arrangement. Taking small sprigs of foliage, cover the floral foam liberally, making sure that you use a good mixture of variegated leaves and berries. Place them in even clumps.

3 Add sprigs of the ornamental chili peppers and rambutans. Both of these

are available as cut flowers on stems. Heavy florist's wire was pushed into the tamarillos, but you could use cocktail sticks if you prefer. Other suitable fruits for a festive arrangement are red grapes, red apples, kumquats, pomegranates, Cape gooseberries (*Physalis*), or you could use dried pine cones as an alternative.

Add the larch twigs, which have small cones attached to them (*right*). Cut down the amaryllis stems, making sure that you keep the flower clusters intact, and place them very carefully in the floral foam so the flowerheads nestle among the foliage. Take care not to allow the pollen to spoil the petals or delicate objects – if necessary, you should remove the stamens.

Amaryllis originate from the damp tropical and subtropical rain forests of South America and the Caribbean. Today, they are mainly cultivated in the Netherlands, although smaller quantities are grown for limited seasons in other regions. The original cultivars were developed mainly in the United Kingdom and are now available in shades of white, pink and red, and also two tones of these colours. Occasionally, the flowers are unsuccessfully dyed yellow.

The flowers are cut while still in bud but showing colour, and are transported to their destination in special, chilled containers. There are several grades of flower, which usually refer to the number of flowerheads on the stem – three is a middle grade and five

is the best. The small bouquets of amaryllis which are often sold in cellophane are normally of poor quality and can be a false economy. Generally, when you think you are buying flowers at a bargain price, unless too many have been produced and the market has been flooded, the reason for the low price may be that the quality is not very high.

The most common amaryllis is 'Red Lion', which is very useful for large, dramatic Christmas arrangements. My favourite amaryllis are the very deep crimson and velvety-textured 'Red Velvet' and 'Liberty', which look festive when mixed with holly (*Ilex*) berries and larch (*Larix*) twigs (*see page 120*). In the spring I prefer to use 'Apple Blossom', which is pale pink and white

and mixes well with blossom (*Prunus*), the lime green of guelder roses (*Viburnum opulus*) and bells of Ireland (*Moluccella laevis*). Both this variety and the dark pink 'Hercules' are very widely available. The peach 'Rilona' is difficult to combine with other flowers because it is an unusual shade; I prefer to enliven it with *Strelitzia* and burnt orange lilies (*Lilium*) such as 'Monte Negro'. All amaryllis can last well, sometimes for up to two or three weeks, so buy your blooms a long time in advance of a party or wedding if you wish them to be fully open for your special celebration.

'Ludwig Dazzler' and 'Mont Blanc' are both white varieties and they mix well in any combination, as shown above.

Amaryllis stems can be cut down for smaller arrangements and make stunning focal flowers for Christmas wreaths. Conveniently, when the *Hippeastrum* varieties are not available, smaller varieties arrive on the market. The miniature amaryllis is known as *Valotta speciosa*. It bears up to five scarlet flowers, which are 3–4 inches (7.5–10 cm) long, per stem, and is in season between August and September. Like its amaryllis cousins, it makes an attractive houseplant.

Left: Because of their large heads, amaryllis tend to be used for big displays, but they are very useful as filler flowers for smaller arrangements. Here, peach 'Rilona' amaryllis are used with berried *Celastrus orbiculatus*, eucalyptus (*Eucalyptus*) pods, *Cotinus*, *Viburnum tinus* and gerberas (*Gerbera*).

Above: 'Ludwig Dazzler' amaryllis has a green centre and is ideal for large displays in winter when there is little else available. Here, it is shown with lilac (*Syringa vulgaris*), blossom (*Prunus glandulosa* 'Alboplena'), larch (*Larix*), broom (*Genista*), ivy (*Hedera*) trails and spruce (*Picea glauca*).

Right: The mauve anemone (*Anemone*) Mona Lisa 'Orchid'.

Above, from left to right: The white anemone Mona Lisa 'White'; the red anemone Mona Lisa 'Red'; a black-eyed white anemone. The Mona Lisa anemones are cultivated from seed and are favoured by flower arrangers because they have large flowerheads. They are rapidly upstaging the De Caen varieties which are cultivated from corms.

ANEMONE

These jewel-coloured flowers belong to my favourite family of Ranunculaceae. The anemone has always been held sacred to love and, according to Greek myth, the scarlet anemone (*Anemone coronaria*) was created by Aphrodite from the blood of her dead lover, Adonis, thus ensuring that he would live forever as a flower. Anemones also appear at the foot of the Cross in some paintings of the Crucifixion. The word "anemone" is thought to be a corruption of Nemesis, the goddess of retribution. It also comes from *anemos*, the Greek name for the wind, from which it takes its common name of windflower. The cultivated varieties of anemone have no scent although, according to early records, old-fashioned varieties must have been very fragrant. A Welsh tradition warned of planting the flowers on graves because they were too aromatic.

s

TABLE ARRANGEMENT WITH ANEMONES

MATERIALS

Small ceramic container

Floral foam tape

Ivy (*Hedera*) berries

Hypericum (*Hypericum*) berries

Viburnum opulus berries

'Gloria Mundi' spray roses (*Rosa*)

Bouvardia 'Joreda'

Red and white 'Striped' anemones

  (*Anemone*)

'Red' Mona Lisa anemones

1 Make sure that your container has been thoroughly cleaned with bleach, then fill it with cold water. Construct a supportive mesh with strips of floral foam tape across the top of the container. If you wish, you could use sticky tape for a large container.

2 Position the ivy and hypericum berries through the mesh to create a good, all-round posy shape suitable for a centre piece. These two berried foliages are being cultivated for an ever-longer season and are available for at least six months of the year to satisfy the current demand for very attractive foliage.

3 Add the viburnum berries and the spray roses. 'Gloria Mundi' is an old-fashioned double shrub rose. It has a twin sister called 'Dorus Rijkers' with the same markings in pale peach. These old-fashioned varieties are very

much in vogue. Add the *Bouvardia*, which should have been well conditioned first in a special *Bouvardia* flower-food. This flower has the reputation of being disappointing, but if it has been properly conditioned by a florist, or by yourself, it will last for between 18 and 22 days. Ask for the flower-food when purchasing the *Bouvardia* and avoid buying it in mixed bunches from supermarkets unless it has the proper flower-food attached.

Add the other flowers, maintaining a domed shape with good variations in the flowers and foliage throughout (*right*). The berries look particularly good if they are positioned to droop over the side of the container. A small arrangement like this is easy to make for a gift and would be a very suitable present for a man because of its bold colouring and strong flower shapes.

The first perennial anemone, A. *coronaria*, was woven into garlands by the Romans and was probably first introduced to Britain during the Roman occupation. In the seventeenth century, the double varieties became very popular during the European craze for bulbs. In a less ardent form of "tulipomania", the plants changed hands at surprisingly high prices. In Britain, it was believed that the first spring-gathered anemones worn against the skin would keep the wearer safe from pestilence for the year.

The De Caen single corm variety, which was developed from

A. *coronaria*, was immensely popular in the

seventeenth century and remained

so until recently, when the plants were largely replaced in popularity by the Mona Lisa varieties. These plants are grown from seed and are taller, with larger flower-heads, than De Caen anemones. The French and Italians grow the very best cut flower anemones, and the huge wholesale market at Rungis, outside Paris, is a good place to admire these beautiful flowers.

De Caen and Mona Lisa anemones are both available from November until the end of June, but are at their best from December to March, with February being the best month for anemones grown on the French and Italian Rivieras. These flowers are available in single-colour bunches in shades of scarlet, magenta, crimson, mauve, purple, lavender and white, and in mixed-coloured bunches. They are either sold in bud or when they are showing colour. The colour of anemones can be enhanced by dunking the flowerhead in water before the conditioning process. To condition them, cut at least 1 inch (2.5 cm) off the stems at an angle, then place in a solution of tepid water and flower-food. If the stems are bent when you buy them, do not worry as they will straighten during conditioning. On average, anemones have a vase life of five days but they may last for as long as eight. Check the level of the water frequently because they are heavy drinkers and will take up large quantities of liquid after a long journey out of water. Anemones tend to curve toward the light, so try to place them in an evenly lit position. Once they have been in water they will not travel particularly well out of water, and their black stamens will shed, so be careful when placing them on a white tablecloth or a delicate surface which could be damaged.

Left: The jewel-like colours of anemones are irresistible massed in a low arrangement on their own, without any further foliage.

Above: This hand-tied posy of Mona Lisa 'White' anemones has been trimmed to fit a glass cube and to stand above it in a wigwam design. Skeletonized leaves were carefully stuck to the lower half of the vase with double-sided adhesive tape to give this pale, ethereal effect.

RAN

UNCULUS

Left: The striped pink and white Ranobelle strain of *Ranunculus*.

Above, from left to right: The salmon-coloured *R.* 'Ranobelle Zalm'; a dark rose ranunculus; a deep yellow ranunculus; the *R. asiaticus* which is grown in the South of England and is sold in short, multi-coloured bunches of ten. The previous three flowers are sold in single-colour bunches of ten and are mainly from the European Riviera. Israel and Southern California also cultivate ranunculus.

The buttercup family of Ranunculaceae is not particularly large but it does contain a great variety of plants, among which are some of my favourites. Undoubtedly my most cherished flowers are ranunculus (*Ranunculus asiaticus*). They are sometimes called Persian, Turban or French buttercups and are direct relatives of the golden-yellow common buttercup (*R. acris*), which is regarded as a weed. I think ranunculus are divine and I adore receiving them for my birthday in late April, when they are plentiful and in season. I prefer them in mixed colours, especially when they are arranged in dazzling combinations, and the short, multi-coloured varieties grown in the South of England are simply breathtaking. These peony-shaped flowers have a bright and fluffy texture and grow in white and every shade of yellow, orange, peach, pink, red, burgundy and purple.

I first discovered the cultivated varieties of ranunculus in the window of a flower shop in St Moritz, Switzerland. At the time, I only dreamt of becoming a florist and every flower shop was a mesmerizing delight. I gazed at the ranunculus, never before having seen such bright colours which clashed, yet looked good together. There is an excellent lesson to be learned from these flowers – if you do it boldly, you can mix colours that you would not have imagined putting together.

It is magnificent to see these flowers growing in fields. In southern Europe, ranunculus are usually grown under glass or polythene, but in California I found the most stunning rainbow of them in a field in Carlsbad, outside San Diego. These striped fields blazed with the largest and most spectacular flowers – their heads almost the size of peonies – that I had ever set eyes on. Generally, strains developed in California are the best ranunculus to buy; the Tecolote strain contains the best and largest flowers for garden flowering. Although all the colours are spectacular, the white variety is pure and beautiful for wedding work and looks lovely when combined with early spring foliage. The yellow varieties are perfect for any spring assembly and the red ranunculus are popular at Christmas – especially when mixed with anemones (*Anemone*) – when they first appear on the market.

Although their natural season is spring, these modern hybrids are grown under glass for about six months of the year. They appear at the end of November and flower until May. Recently, the Ranobelle series of ranunculus, which is grown from seed rather than tuber, has been grown commercially. The flowerheads are larger than those of other strains – about 3 inches (7.5 cm) across – and the colours are much brighter and bolder. The flowers are also available earlier in the season. The most important development is the firmer stems, which are not hollow like the traditional varieties. These have the advantage of allowing the flower to drink more freely and consequently last longer. Ranobelle ranunculus are also less susceptible to the gray mould *botrytis* than their older relatives. These flowers benefit from being transported in water, so if you are purchasing them as a gift you should ask your florist to "aqua-pack" them. This involves creating a receptacle for water at the base of a tied bunch.

Above: Yellow striped ranunculus from Italy.

Right: A formal Victorian posy-style arrangement of ranunculus, guelder roses (*Viburnum opulus*), snowdrops (*Galanthus*) and ivy (*Hedera*) leaves.

CELEBRATION SWAG WITH RANUNCULUS

1

2

3

MATERIALS

Prunus glandulosa 'Alboplena'

Prunus triloba

Budded camellia (*Camellia*) foliage

A wire-edged plastic tie or string

Guelder roses (*Viburnum opulus*)

Pink ranunculus (*Ranunculus*)

Lilac (*Syringa vulgaris*

'Ruhm von Horstenstein')

Silk taffeta ribbon

1 This swag would be suitable for a big celebration such as a wedding, where a round top table could be given a special decoration. If you do not wish to decorate every chair around the table, you could decorate alternate ones instead. To start, take a few tall stems of *Prunus* and a spray of camellia foliage. Bind their stems with a long wire-edged plastic tie or with string.

2 Add the guelder roses, which fill the swag and give the arrangement body. Bear in mind that you do not want the swag to be too flat so you need to find foliage and flowers that are rounded. Secure the stems of the flowers with another bind of string or plastic tie.

3 Continue to add the flowers, placing the ranunculus and lilac throughout the arrangement. Make sure that the swag has a good shape when viewed from all sides. Select flowers and foliage to suit their position in the arrangement – in other words, if they flow to the left then you should place them on that side. Bind the stems very tightly, and tie securely. Trim the ends of the plastic tie or string.

This type of swag could be hung downward, with the bow at the top, as on a pew end. Or, you can hang it the right way up, as I have done here, with the bow at the bottom (*right*). Firmly tie the base of the swag to the chair with string, and also anchor it higher up to stop it flopping forward. Tie the ribbon in a lavish bow. If the caterers will be supplying the chairs, check with them first that these will have open backs to which you can tie the swags. The gold chairs which are often used by catering and banqueting firms provide an excellent framework for this style of swag.

Generally, these flowers require no special conditioning other than being given a deep drink of water when you first get them, and will last for up to three weeks. They bloom well without flower-food, provided their lower foliage is removed and they are given plenty of fresh water at regular intervals – they are heavy drinkers. Their stems curve to meet the light and will move around in the warmth of an interior room. These flowers improve with age; they know the secret of growing old gracefully and show their full character at the end of their lives. The buds are bowl-shaped, then they often open out flat like anemones when fully open and can be mistaken for them or for poppies (*Papaver*). Some writers have described the ranunculus as the ugly duckling of the flower kingdom; unpromising, wizened bulbs sprout the most beautiful, showy blooms. They may also look very droopy before they have been conditioned, but by the next day they will have perked up to show their alluring shapes and colours.

Ranunculus were first introduced to Europe from the Orient as far back as the thirteenth century. By the seventeenth century, ranunculus, anemones, tulips (*Tulipa*), pinks (*Dianthus*) and auriculas (*Primula auricula*) had all become what were known as florist's flowers. In those days, a florist was someone (usually rich) who bred and exhibited flowers – it was only after the Industrial Revolution, in the late nineteenth century, that growing prized flowers became more wide-spread. Throughout the eighteenth century, ranunculus were popular and William Cobbett, famous for his book *Rural Rides*, wrote extensively about their cultivation. In the early nineteenth century, many ranunculus were growing in England and the English florists produced new striped and marked variations from seed. After that, they declined in popularity and it is only recently that they have regained their status as commercial cut flowers and garden plants.

Left: This spring arrangement uses a basket of twigs, on a wire mesh base, into which I fitted a container of water. South African poker reeds were arranged between the container and the wire mesh. I covered the twigs in moss, then placed *Lachenaria* 'Quadricolor' around the mossy bottom and filled the middle of the arrangement with crown imperials (*Fritillaria imperialis*) and buttercup-yellow ranunculus.

Above: This tree was created with my favourite English ranunculus (*Ranunculus asiaticus*). An old tree branch was cemented into a pot and flowers, twigs and moss were pinned to the floral foam ball at the top. Bunches of ranunculus were placed in floral foam at the base of the tree.

Above, from left to right: *Papaver somniferum* 'Hen and Chickens'; *P. s.* 'Red Peony'. The seed heads of poppy flowers are extremely useful for giving form and texture to fresh and dried arrangements.

P O P P I E S

Poppies are among the most loved and cherished plants of all because of their bold colours and delicate petals. There is nothing as breathtaking as the sight of the blue Himalayan poppy (*Meconopsis*) flourishing in a garden, the mix of colour and the wonderfully curved stems of a vase of Oriental poppies (*Papaver orientale*) or the beauty and simplicity of crimson field poppies (*P. rhoeas*). Sadly, most poppies are short-lived, both in their natural habitat and as cut flowers. A beautiful poppy flowering in the garden one day will have shed all its petals by the following morning. For this reason it is entirely appropriate that the field poppy should be the flower of remembrance, with its red petals symbolizing the dead of two World Wars.

Left: A fully opened Oriental poppy (*P. orientale* 'Allegro Viva') in all its

splendour. It is the poppy of the traditional garden border.

The poppy family, Papaveraceae, is relatively small by most standards in the plant kingdom, and the majority of the species is distributed primarily in the northern hemisphere, but some poppies do grow in South Africa and South America. The field poppy is the most common variety, and is generally found on cultivated ground, such as wheat fields where the soil has been disturbed. I think these must be the flowers described in the Bible as "the lilies of the field", for they are the ones that stain the fields of the countryside, and brighten the roadside verges. Yet this once familiar plant has now become drastically reduced in numbers and should not be picked in the wild any more; modern farming practices and the widespread use of herbicides still pose a threat to the cheerful, scarlet field poppy.

Although poppies look very fragile they can survive in infertile and harsh conditions, and are fully hardy. Many poppies can be grown from seed (although Oriental poppies and their cultivars are best propagated from root cuttings) and will thrive in any well-drained soil. Most species have well-developed leafy stems, although the ones most commonly sold as cut flowers, such as the Iceland poppy (*P. nudicaule*), have leafless, hairy stems. The flowers in the poppy family are generally showy, attractive and brightly coloured, and the seed head or ovary which holds the fruit of the plant is useful for flower arranging, whether it is used fresh or dried. Each variety of poppy has its own distinctive seed head.

Poppies are often believed to be unreliable as cut flowers, and this is certainly true of wild poppies and garden varieties because they shed their petals so quickly. However, there are some exceptions and these are sold as cut flowers throughout the world. They include the very popular Oriental poppy, which was first cultivated in France although it originally came from Iran. Traditionally, it had orangey-red petals with a black centre, but it now has many different cultivars. The most popular Iceland poppy is called 'San Remo', and is named very appropriately after the area from which many poppies are harvested for sale in Europe; the French and Italian Rivieras produce poppies from February to August. Cultivated Iceland poppies can last for between six and nine days, while Oriental poppies only tend to last for between four and seven days.

Above: A vase of burnt orange Iceland poppies (*P. nudicaule*).
Right: Iceland poppies mixed with laurustinus (*Viburnum tinus*) berries and kumquat foliage. The floral foam is camouflaged with carpet moss, held in place with wire bent into pins.

POPPIES AND PASTA CENTRE PIECE

MATERIALS

Rectangular glass container

Sheets of multi-coloured dried pasta

Sheet of bubble wrap or plastic

Floral foam

Knife

Pair of sharp scissors

Double-sided adhesive tape

Variegated ivy (*Hedera*) leaves

Sprig of carpet moss

Florist's wire

Iceland poppies (*Papaver nudicaule*)

1 This is a centre piece for a dinner party, which is why pasta has been used. A similar effect could be created with alternate pieces of dried egg and spinach lasagne. Line the inside of the glass container with sheets of the dried pasta. Push down the plastic carefully to hold the pasta in place. Bubble wrap is superior to ordinary plastic because it cushions the pasta and protects it from the moisture in the floral foam.

2 Cut the floral foam to fit the shape snugly, soak in water, then place in the container. Trim the bubble wrap and tuck it in around the floral foam. Make sure that the foam sits higher than the vase, so that you will be able to make the flowers and foliage hang down over the edge of the container to soften its appearance.

3 Cut some large, glossy ivy leaves from their stems, leaving long stalks which you push into the floral foam. Make sure that you cover all the foam,

then add some carpet moss along the top, pinning it in place with florist's wire bent into hairpins or bobby pins.

Arrange the fully opened Iceland poppies in a linear fashion (*right*). This type of arrangement is called vegetative because it is similar to the way that poppies grow. When they are sold as cut flowers, Iceland poppies will have been post-harvest treated and their stems sealed to prevent sap loss. If you have to cut them down to fit this arrangement, you must reseal their stems. To do this, singe their cut stems with the flame from a candle. As this is an arrangement for a celebration, we have used floral foam but this means that the flowers may not last for more than a couple of days. Take care to hold the base of the poppy stems when inserting them in the floral foam as otherwise they may snap. Any buds are unlikely to open in the foam so you may prefer to use opened flowers.

Most poppies lose a lot of sap when cut and will soon wilt unless the ends of their stems are sealed. You can do this by burning the ends with a match or lighter. This process keeps the stems turgid and upright, and prevents the petals wilting. Poppies are best cut just before the buds burst open; they will last longer this way and it is great fun to watch them unfolding. If they are harvested when too young, the buds will not open at all, so make sure that you can see some petal colour showing through the buds before you cut them or buy them from a florist. The buds have a hairy casing, with two lobes which part to release the papery petals. When the flower opens, the lobes fall to the ground.

One of the most commonly grown and best-loved of these flowers is the opium poppy (*P. somniferum*), which is a delight for gardeners with its shiny blooms and subtle variations in colour. It is almost certain that the opium poppy was first cultivated for its seed in Neolithic times, while the Ancient Egyptians definitely knew about its narcotic properties because they used it as a drug to induce sleep. However, it was the Arabs who popularized the use of the opium derived from the poppy. They have named the flower "the father of sleep". The seeds of the opium poppy are also used as a garnish for breads and salads, and in oil cake which is made for cattle.

The opium poppy is one of my favourite flowers, but sadly it does not travel well when cut. However, it makes up for this by producing some very attractive seed heads. The stems of seed heads do not need to be sealed with flame but you should cut at least 1 inch (2.5 cm) off the base of the stem at an angle, then place it in fresh water into which flower-food has been dissolved. As a rule, the varieties of poppy with the best seed heads are very leafy, and any foliage that will sit below the water line should be removed to stop it becoming slimy and making the water murky.

The best time to gather poppy seed heads from the garden is when they are fully matured and have shed their petals. They can be hung upside down in bunches and air-dried in a warm room or airing cupboard, but first you should shake out the seeds otherwise they will scatter in all directions when you hang up the poppies. Keep these seeds in a dry place if you wish to sow them the following year. The 'Giganteum' variety has swollen seed heads which are often available as dried flowers. One rather eccentric variety is known as 'Hen and Chickens', and this produces seed heads which look deformed. The main seed head is surrounded by a halo of smaller seed heads, and is a novelty much enjoyed by flower arrangers in both its fresh and dried forms.

Left: Here, a front-facing arrangement has been created with *P. somniferum* 'Hen and Chickens', arum lily flowers and foliage (*Zantedeschia*), small purple chives (*Allium*) and *A. schubertii*, 'La Reve' lilies (*Lilium*), cuckoo pint (*Arum italicum*) and artichokes (*Cynara scolymus*).

Above: I used poppy and scabious (*Scabiosa*) seed heads, hydrangea (*Hydrangea*) heads, feverfew (*Matricaria*), mint (*Mentha* 'Jocka'), marjoram (*Origanum*), borage (*Borago*), green dill (*Anethum graveolens*), ornamental cabbage leaves, chive flowers (*Allium*), yellow scabious (*Scabiosa*), *Curcuma*, 'Sterling Silver' roses (*Rosa*), *Iris hoogiana*, *Craspedia globosa* and swirls of grasses for this herbal cottage garden wreath.

RCISSUS

Left: 'Paper White' narcissus (*Narcissus*) are cultivated for their scent and grown in Israel, Italy and Japan.

Above, from left to right: 'Carlton', a traditional daffodil; the double-flowered 'Tahiti'; the sweetly scented

jonquil 'Suzy'. These old-fashioned double and scented varieties are currently very popular.

Even though they are seasonal, daffodils are among the world's top five best-selling flowers and, in the

United Kingdom, they are number one. The Welsh regard them as their national flower and wear them as

buttonholes on St David's Day. The botanical name for daffodils is *Narcissus*, after the Greek youth who was

transformed into a flower by the gods because he was obsessed with his appearance. The name is also

thought to be related to the Greek word *narkos*, which means to stun and intoxicate, and certainly some of

the varieties have a strong and heavenly scent. Although the whole family shares the same botanical name,

the single-flowered variety is called a daffodil, while the complex and multi-headed varieties are known as

narcissus or are identified by their variety name. The scented narcissus have brief lives as cut flowers

because they expend all their energy on producing their perfume.

It was the Romans who first cultivated wild narcissus, and the popularity of these flowers has grown steadily ever since, with new varieties being developed every year. Daffodils were mentioned in early medieval records of monasteries and apothecaries. From the sixteenth century onward, written records show how interest in these flowers grew in Europe, especially in the Netherlands, with doubles being the variety most highly prized by collectors. The public seems to have an almost insatiable appetite for these flowers and more daffodils are planted each year than any other perennial ornamental plant. The United Kingdom is a major exporter of narcissus, both as bulbs and cut flowers, and is followed by the United States, Canada, Australia, New Zealand and the Netherlands.

Left: 'Paper White' narcissus arranged in a similar way to their natural habitat, with bun moss.
Above: A woodland arrangement with large pieces of bark, shiitake mushrooms, *Eucalyptus gomphocephala*, and 'Tahiti' and 'Barrett Browning' narcissus.

The narcissus family is divided into eight major groups which are distinguished by their flower shapes: large corolla (trumpet) varieties such as the popular golden-yellow 'Carlton'; short corolla varieties such as 'Verger'; double-flowering varieties, which I love, such as 'Dick Wilden' and 'Golden Ducat'; jonquils, which are the sweetly scented members of the family; polyanthus cultivars which are also scented, such as 'Paper White' and the multi-headed 'Geranium'; tazetta varieties which are strongly scented too,

such as 'Minnow'; poeticus narcissus which are small, such as 'Actaea'; and split corolla varieties, such as 'Spleetkronig', which have a frilled corolla. This latter variety is gaining in popularity because it has a delightful, old-fashioned look.

The life of any cut narcissus is about five days, unless purchased at the bud or "pencil stage" when it may last for up to seven days. One often sees narcissus for sale in boxes on market stalls, and this does them no harm as they will last for up to a week without water. When you use them, cut at least 1 inch (2.5 cm) off the stems. Narcissus need to be conditioned carefully because they excrete latex, also known as daffodil slime, which can be detrimental to the life of other cut flowers. You can buy a special preservative that allows you to mix narcissus with other flowers without any harm coming to them. However, this is not necessary as all you need to do is leave the narcissus, for 24 hours, in water to which you have added a drop of bleach. After this, you can combine them with other flowers. Reputable florists will have already conditioned their narcissus in a professional manner, so you should have no problems in mixing them with other spring flowers such as ranunculus (*Ranunculus*) or anemones (*Anemone*), although the narcissus may die first.

HAND-TIED NARCISSUS BOUQUET

MATERIALS

Pair of sharp secateurs

Ivy (*Hedera*) berries

Witch hazel (*Hamamelis mollis*)

Laurustinus (*Viburnum tinus*) berries

Guelder roses (*V. opulus* 'Roseum')

'Soleil d'Or' narcissus (*Narcissus*)

'Pearl' narcissus

'Suzy' narcissus

String or raffia

Clematis (*Clematis*) vine

Hank of raffia

1 Cut down the foliage stems to about 7 inches (17.5 cm) and strip the bottom of the stems of all leaves and buds. Arrange seven stems of foliage in your hand as a starting point for the hand-tied bouquet.

2 Add the narcissus in groups of three because these flowers are quite dainty and will be lost if put into the bouquet singly. Make sure that you arrange the stems in a spiral so the point where you hold them is the narrowest. This is essential because it enables you to use more plant material than you could normally hold in one hand. There should be no foliage on the stems at this binding point, and certainly none beneath it. You can bind the bouquet with string or raffia here before adding more material if you wish, but I prefer not to because this makes a lighter, looser bunch which

looks more natural. It also gives you the opportunity to add or take out plant material as you see fit.

3 Continue adding material to the bouquet, making sure that you get a good variety of foliage all around the bunch. The witch hazel gives height, while filler flowers such as the guelder roses need to be placed lower down because they are flatter and fluffier.

4 Try to hold the flowers in as relaxed a way as possible to avoid damaging the stems. Continue to add them to the bouquet until you are happy with the shape, then tie at the binding point with string or raffia. Add the clematis vine in loops around the bouquet and secure with more string or raffia.

Make a lavish bow with one-third of a hank of raffia, trim the ends, then attach it to the front of the bouquet with more raffia (*right*).

DELPHIN

IUMS

Left: *Delphinium* 'Purple Sky'. Cut delphinium flowers are usually ordered by their colour and length of stem.

Above, from left to right: 'Sandpiper' is white with a black eye; the pink 'Princess Caroline'.

The modern delphinium is often thought of as a lovely old-fashioned garden plant whose tall spires are perfect for cottage gardens and whose blue flowers dominate summer borders. However, the modern delphinium has been specially created, and over 150 years of hybridizing mean that it no longer bears any relation to its ancestors. The love and enthusiasm of many breeders for the blue spires have produced the magnificent blooms that we can obtain as cut flowers and also grow in garden borders, where I think they are unsurpassed.

The Greeks and Romans were the first to be interested in delphiniums but it was the medicinal quality of *Delphinium staphisagria* that concerned them, because it is an antidote to scorpion bites. The name "delphinium" comes from the Greek word for dolphin, as the unopened buds were thought to resemble these creatures. It was not until the sixteenth century that delphiniums were grown for their beauty.

The colour spectrum of delphiniums is vast, ranging from white and cream to blue, mauve, violet, pink and purple; each floret has either a white or a black centre. About 50 varieties are sold as cut flowers, and new ones are developed each year for both decorative use as cut flowers and also as cultivars for gardens. One of the most startling delphiniums is the peachy pink 'Princess Caroline', which was named after Princess Caroline of Monaco. Its colour was achieved by crossing *D. consolida* with the rock plant *D. nudicaule*. This peachy pink delphinium is perfectly matched by the peach rose 'Dorus Rijkers' and I once had the pleasure of using both these flowers for a royal birthday ball. I am particularly fond of a green delphinium known as 'Gossamer' which makes an elegant contrast to the blue variety 'Skyline' and the cream and white varieties.

Blue flowers are always popular as a gift for men and from my observations in my shop I have noticed that men often buy them for their brilliant colours and hues. Blue flowers are rare, and the wide range of blue that is available from the delphinium hybrids is breathtaking. You can find sky blue, cornflower blue, Wedgwood blue, mid-blue, dark blue, lilac blue and even two-tone effects of blue and mauve such as those seen in 'Spindrift' and 'Blue Dawn'. The best way to purchase a particular colour is to find a reference or to provide a piece of ribbon or fabric in the shade you are looking for. Sadly, the full range of colours is only available for a very limited season and can rarely be guaranteed even then, so you may have to be flexible when ordering the flowers.

Above: Delphiniums are either sold in self-colour or mixed-colour bunches of five. Here, a mixed bunch has been arranged with *Eryngium maritimum* 'Orion'.

Right: For a large proportion of the year, blue bee (*Delphinium x belladonna* 'Volkerfrieden') is widely cultivated and less expensive than the hybrid varieties. Here it is arranged simply with cream lisianthus (*Eustoma russellianum*). The base of the urn contains mind-your-own-business (*Helxine soleirolii*).

delphiniums

Right: Delphiniums, both hybrid and belladonna, are best arranged with other seasonal flowers and foliage.

Burgundy stocks (*Matthiola incana*), white *Trachelium caeruleum* 'Album' and lilac lisianthus (*Eustoma russellianum*) are all

complemented by the lime green spires of bells of Ireland (*Moluccella laevis*).

delphiniums

Above: To make delphiniums look more contemporary, a silk fabric container has been used with a cylinder lining and the flowers are mixed with tropical anthuriums (*Anthurium*), shampoo gingers (*Zingiber spectabile* 'Griff') and trailing morning glory vine (*Ipomoea hederacea*). The rose (*Rosa*) is 'Yellow Success' and the chrysanthemum (*Chrysanthemum*) is 'Hoof Lane'.

Colour is seasonal and I think everyone has ideas about which colours appeal to them at different times of the year. In the spring we long for yellow to brighten the days, as summer unfolds we turn more to ßpinks and reds, and later in the summer we enjoy blues for their coolness and because they reflect blue summer skies. By the time autumn or fall comes we are ready for deeper colour, and I always sell more deep red and orange flowers at this time of year. The hanging ball shown on pages 162–3 uses delphiniums in a seasonal way.

It is best to buy delphiniums when the lower six or seven flowers are open. Cut at least 1 inch (2.5 cm) off the stems at an angle and place in water mixed with flower-food. It is always best to transport delphiniums in water otherwise they will soon dry out and shrivel up. Sometimes the florets are too heavy for the stems, in which case the hollow stems can be strengthened by inserting a thin stick inside them. Traditionally, delphinium stems were held upside down, filled with water and then plugged with cotton wool to give them strength. However, this is a complicated process and very often the stems will break while you are trying to strengthen them.

It is best to buy delphiniums which have been post-harvest treated in a solution of silver nitrate, otherwise they will only last for a few days. When you get the flowers, leave them in their protective wrappers but cut at least 1 inch (2.5 cm) off the stems at an angle, then place the flowers in water and flower-food. If the delphiniums are not wrapped, use a high-sided container to support their stems. The foliage looks unimpressive so strip off all the lower leaves. Delphiniums are very poisonous and are also very sensitive to ethylene gas which ages them, so they should never be stored with fruit and vegetables which exude this.

Above: Delphiniums are excellent for wiring. Here, florets have been wired into a head-dress with poppy (*Papaver*) seed heads, *Senecio*, 'Henri Matisse' roses (*Rosa*) and *Allium*.
Left: For an informal table arrangement, cut delphinium spires into short lengths and arrange with *Moluccella*, *Alchemilla*, *Nigella* and bundles of asparagus and lavender (*Lavandula*).

HANGING DELPHINIUM BALL

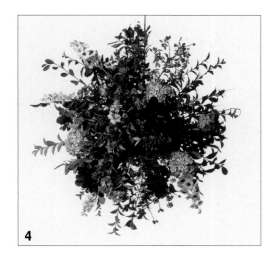

MATERIALS

1 box of floral foam

2 large hanging basket frames

Heavy florist's wire

Heavy-duty rope

Wide-gauged wire mesh

Selection of foliage

White 'Sandpiper' and lilac

 'Arrow' delphiniums (*Delphinium*)

Hydrangea (*Hydrangea*) heads

'Yellow Success' roses (*Rosa*)

1 Using a large bucket or container, soak a box of floral foam thoroughly. Shape the blocks into circles and place in each hanging basket. To create a hanging ball, you need to wire the two hanging baskets together to make a tough, spherical container which will support the weight of the floral foam, flowers and foliage. Knot the rope securely to the top of the hanging ball.

2 Cover the ball with wire mesh to keep the two halves together, increase the strength of the ball and keep the

floral foam intact. At this stage, you can place the ball in water for a further soaking if you wish.

3 Establish a round shape with the foliage. I have used *Cotinus*, privet, *Cotoneaster* and rose hips (*Rosa canina*). You need to hang up the ball at a comfortable height for working, ideally in the position in which it will eventually hang. You need strong girders from which to hang the ball, because it is extremely heavy when full of water and plant material. If hanging one in a marquee, ask the supplier to provide a suitable construction. Make sure that you have covered the floral foam before adding the flowers.

4 Add delphiniums to establish the outline and insert the hydrangeas deeper in the arrangement. It is important to add most of the delphiniums at the last stage because they are quite fragile. They should have been well-conditioned and you will need to hold them at their bases to avoid them snapping when you insert them in the floral foam. Check the shape from all sides and from a distance.

Add the roses (*right*) and mist well before raising the ball into position. Keep a plastic sheet under the ball for several hours to catch the water drips.

Right: *Iris oncocyclus atropurpurea* is an unusual black iris which is grown extensively in Israel in early spring.

Above, from left to right: The widow iris, sometimes called the snake's head iris (*Hermodactylus tuberosus*) is by far my favourite; a common commercial iris, 'Blue Magic'; *Iris reticulata* 'Danfordiae'; *I. reticulata* 'J. S. Dijt'. *I. reticulata* was one of the favourites of Vita Sackville-West, creator of the beautiful garden at Sissinghurst Castle in Kent, England, and she commented: "It seems extraordinary that anything so gay, delicate and brilliant should prefer the rigours of winter to the amenities of spring."

I R I S E S

I have to declare that I am not a great fan of the commercial cut flower varieties of iris. I much prefer the early-flowering varieties of *Iris reticulata* and the bearded garden flag irises which, alas, do not last well in water. However, not everyone feels the same way as I do and the iris has many fans – it is an immensely important cut flower and is sold very successfully throughout the world. To the Ancient Greeks, the iris was the emblem of the gods; for the Pharaohs in Egypt it was a regal symbol; and in Europe the iris became a heraldic symbol for chivalry. It was the fleur-de-lis of Louis VII and can be found on all kinds of carvings and embroidered on tapestries of the time. The iris was often painted by the Italian and Dutch masters, and I have been encouraged to look at irises anew because of the works of Monet and Van Gogh.

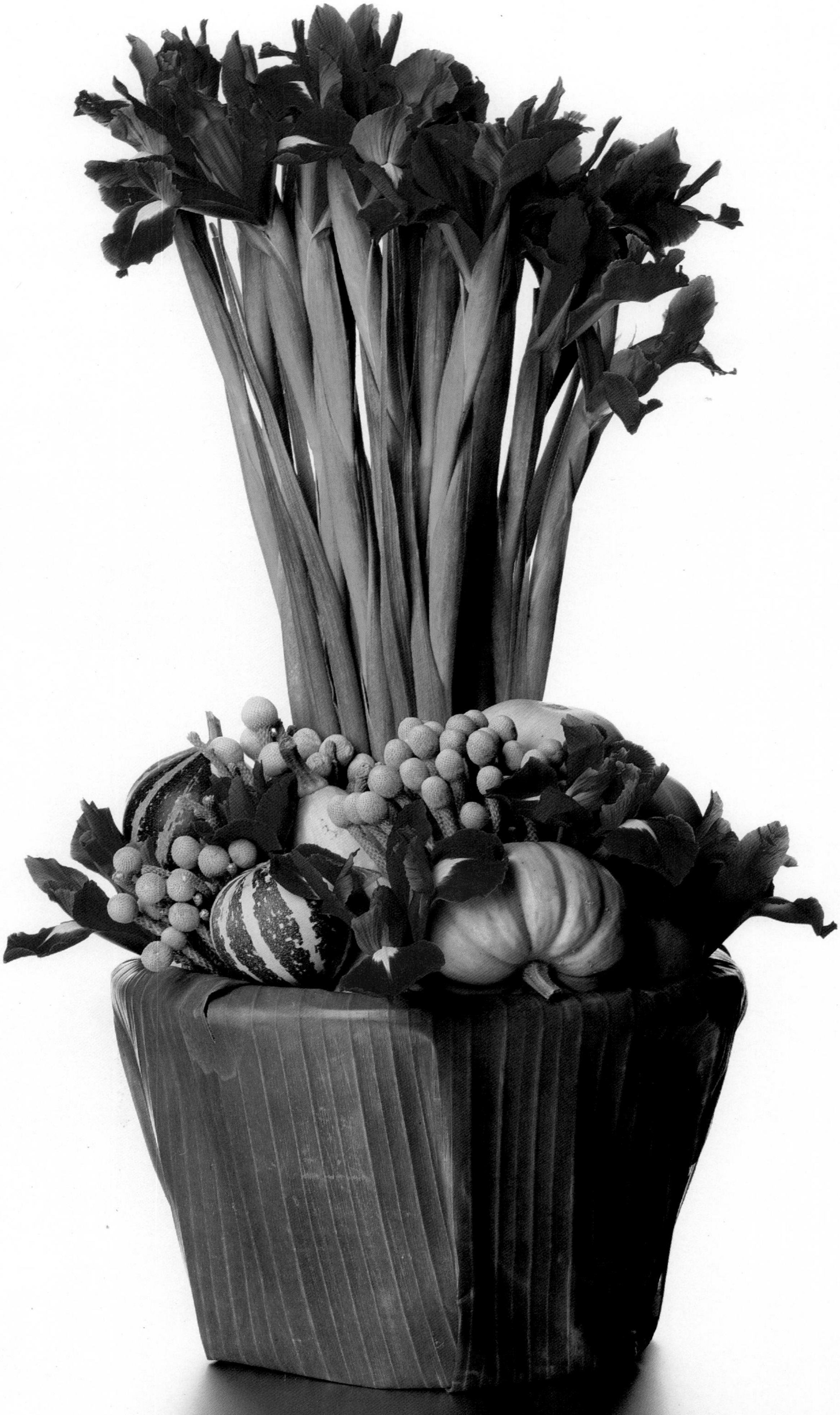

Irises belong to a very large family of flowering plants named Iridaceae which includes ixias (*Ixia*), gladioli (*Gladiolus*), freesias (*Freesia*) and crocuses (*Crocus*). There are about 200 varieties of iris, all of which have the same characteristic "standard" and "fall" petals, even though some irises have bulbs and other varieties have rhizome root systems.

One of the reasons for the popularity of irises is their quirky arrangement of petals. The three petals that grow downward are known as "falls" and balance the three petals, called "standards", that grow upward. Throughout their short lives from pointed bud to full bloom, irises change their physical characteristics which is why people like them, despite their poor longevity. If you purchase a flower and watch it bloom in your own home, you are really witnessing at close quarters one of nature's greatest and most dazzling miracles for yourself.

The arrival of *I. reticulata* each year is always one of the first signs that winter is bidding us farewell and that spring is soon to arrive. The blue and gold flowers will often poke through snow-covered or even frozen ground to greet us after the

gloom of winter. When purchased, the buds should just be coming into flower. These irises are usually sold in bunches of ten, wrapped in paper to avoid dehydration. Often they are still attached to their bulbs, in which case they should be conditioned with the bulbs attached — give them a good drink of warm water and flower-food. They are slightly fragrant and have a short life span of about five to seven days.

The irises which are most commonly used as cut flowers are hybrids of the Spanish iris (*I. xiphium*) yet, confusingly, they are known as "Dutch irises" because they were produced in the Netherlands in the early twentieth century. They are cultivated all the year around, particularly in the Netherlands, Southern France, Italy and on the Isles of Scilly. Most flower-producing regions of the world cultivate irises locally. The largest assortment of irises can be found between March and May. Only buy irises when their buds show a little colour, otherwise they will not open. Irises that are already in flower will not last long and are only worth buying if you need immediate colour or open flowers for an arrangement.

Above: Irises are very popular, and are suitable for minimal arrangements and ikebana (Japanese flower arrangements). Here, two 'Professor Blaauw' irises are arranged with agapanthus (*Agapanthus*) seed heads and a stem of cock's comb (*Celosia*). The stems that run horizontally across the arrangement are cut from agapanthus and are held in place by anchoring them to the back of the celosia with a piece of florist's wire bent into a hairpin or bobby pin.

Left: An arrangement of 'Professor Blaauw' irises with gourds and *Brunia laevis* 'Silver Brunia'. The container was covered with banana (*Ananas*) leaves.

IRISES IN A TWIGGY BASKET

MATERIALS

Watertight container

Birch (*Betula*) twigs

Florist's reel wire

Pair of sharp scissors

Clematis (*Clematis*) vine

Guelder roses (*Viburnum opulus*)

Ivy (*Hedera*) berries

Witch hazel (*Hamamelis mollis*)

Prunus glandulosa 'Alboplena'

Widow irises (*Hermodactylus tuberosus*)

'Blue Magic' irises (*Iris*)

'Ideal' irises

1 I like to create designs in which the container is part of the design, and this is a classic example of this sort of arrangement. You can use any watertight container to create a twig basket. Cut the birch twigs down to an appropriate size and wire them together into tight bunches with florist's reel wire. Start to bind them with more wire onto the outside of the container.

2 Add further bunches of birch twigs as you work around the container until you have covered all of it. Tightly bind the wire around the bottom of the container. Then cut off any twigs and pieces of wire which protrude.

3 Twist clematis vine into the twigs to conceal your wires, tidy up the bottom of the container and soften the base.

4 When you are happy with the shape of the clematis vines, fill the inside of the container with water and start to arrange the flowers and foliage. The lime green guelder roses contrast with the dark green ivy berries. Sprigs of witch hazel and white *Prunus* add height and lighten the arrangement.

Irises are quite dominating flowers, so they look best when arranged on their own. Groups of the widow iris have been placed together so that their green petals will not be lost among the foliage (*right*). The darker blue 'Blue Magic' and the lighter 'Ideal' irises are mixed alternately throughout the arrangement. The flowerheads are kept on the same level as the birch twigs so that the container and flowers become one arrangement. Other suitable varieties of iris which you could use include 'Wedgwood' which, as its name suggests, is the mid-blue of Wedgwood china. 'Purple Sensation' provides a good deep purple and the white 'White Perfection' is often a good length for big arrangements.

S W E E T

Originally from Sicily, the sweet pea (*Lathyrus odoratus*) is a garden flower that has long been prized both in

Europe and the United States for its colour and scent. The butterfly-shaped flowers grow in an abundance

of colours, from red through to deep lilac, as well as all the subtle pastel hues. Sweet peas are fun to grow

from seed, and their lovely fragrance always delights. The older varieties still have the best scent, although

their petals may not be as ruffled as modern plants. Sweet peas are grown commercially both in greenhouses

and outdoors in many flower-producing countries of the world but, sadly, not all commercially grown sweet

peas have a perfume. The European nations – especially the United Kingdom, Italy, Holland and France –

are the most industrious growers of the sweet pea family but, in my opinion, the British growers produce

the best sweet peas in the world. There is an impressive tradition of growing and showing sweet peas in the

United Kingdom, whose flowers are renowned for their length of stem, colour and fragrance.

P E A S

Right: A scented sweet pea,
Lathyrus odoratus 'Blue Danube'.

Left, from left to right: When
grown as cut flowers, sweet peas
are usually referred to by colour
rather than by name. Seed catalogues provide detailed names but
it is almost impossible to order
sweet peas from your florist by
name. Shown here is the soft,
salmony pink 'Band Aid';
'Diamond Wedding'; the bright
pink 'Milestone'; and *Lathyrus
grandiflorus*, which is the everlasting
sweet pea and is generally found
growing in cottage gardens rather
than sold as a cut flower.

171

Above: Sweet peas with double lisianthus (*Eustoma*) and *Alchemilla mollis*. The container was covered with asparagus tips fixed with double-sided tape.

Left: Sweet peas look terrific arranged simply on their own without foliage or other flowers. This arrangement shows their range of colours.

Sweet peas have always been among my favourite flowers, and as a child I cultivated my own little sweet pea patch in the garden – I liked being able to harvest so many different colours each day during sunny periods. The delight of discovering older varieties (*L. latifolius*) in the cottage gardens of relatives is a memory I will always cherish. The wilder varieties of sweet pea have a divine scent and lovely curly vines with long leaf tendrils. In Britain, they grow in woods and hedges, and flower between mid-June and August. They are perennials and are often called everlasting sweet peas.

It is easy to make a stunning arrangement of sweet peas because they look best on their own. They can be bought in mixed-colour bunches but are more commonly graded and sold commercially in single colours. The length of stem is often a fair way to judge the quality of flower, because the best and strongest flowers generally have the longest stems. However, often the best-looking varieties have little or no scent, while the shorter-stemmed ones with few flowerheads per stem have the heaviest perfume. Sweet pea breeders are continually cross-fertilizing flowers to improve both the scent and the number of flowerheads.

Although I loved growing, picking and arranging sweet peas when I was a child, I was always disappointed that they did not last long in water. The most important rule when you arrange sweet peas is not to cram too many together in a vase because they will smother each other and their petals will soon drop. If you are using floral foam, always resubmerge it in water, to which flower-food has been added, before you

173

sweet peas

arrange the flowers. It will then have absorbed the maximum amount of moisture. Sadly, garden-grown sweet peas will not last as long when cut as those grown commercially. This is because commercially grown sweet peas are treated with a special preparation of silver nitrate to reduce the amount of hormones that they exude after harvesting.

All flowers, and not only sweet peas, continue to produce hormones after they have been harvested, but it is one hormone in particular, that is present in ethylene, which determines how long the flowers will last. For some flowers, including sweet peas, carnations (*Dianthus*), snapdragons (*Antirrhinum*) and baby's breath (*Gypsophila*), ethylene is the grim reaper of the flower world. Ethylene gas is made by all plant parts and the richer its concentration, the greater the amount of hormone produced and the shorter the life of the cut flower. Air pollution also contains ethylene, and it builds up on hot days in the city. For this reason, you should beware of buying any flowers that have been exposed to heat or are sold in highly polluted areas such as by the roadside.

Most growers try to combat the production of ethylene by treating cut flowers after they have been harvested. The most commonly used treatment is silver nitrate, which interferes with the action and synthesis of ethylene by the flower. It also contains anti-bacterial agents, thereby preventing bacteria

Left: This exotic party arrangement mixes seasonal fruit and flowers. It contains sweet peas, *Astilbe arendsii*, *Alchemilla mollis*, 'Black Tea' roses (*Rosa*) and *Galax* leaves. It is crowned with a pineapple top, and cherries sit on the lower tier. Spring onions conceal the floral foam at the base.

from building up in the stems of the flowers. A preparation of silver nitrate is mixed with water and the flowers are left in this treatment for about 10 hours. When treated in this way, the life of sweet peas can be prolonged by more than 75 percent. It is not advisable to make up your own solution as it only works when very precise quantities are used.

If not arranged on their own, sweet peas look best mixed with other seasonal flowers, foliage and fruit, and can be used in a diversity of arrangements. As they are midsummer flowers, sweet peas are suitable for light containers made from wicker and glass, and thin wire baskets.

Soft flowers with large petals, such as lisianthus (*Eustoma*), are excellent for mixing with sweet peas. In the arrangement on page 173 I used the double lisianthus (*E. grandiflorum*), which is often mistaken for a sweet pea because it has the same lovely droopy tendrils. Like the sweet pea, lisianthus comes from an arid, warm climate – it was originally found growing in the prairies of Texas. Simple, natural containers are best for these flowers, so I used young asparagus tips and double-sided adhesive tape

to make a seasonal vase (*see page* 50). I mixed lady's mantle (*Alchemilla mollis*) flowers with the sweet peas, although young asparagus foliage would be an equally effective alternative.

Sweet peas are ideal flowers to use in posies because they are light and easy to hold. They are especially effective in wedding posies, and their curly edges give extra texture to Victorian posies. In floristry terms, a Victorian posy has come to mean one consisting of concentric circles of flowers. In the past, these were often wired, but it is very easy to arrange a posy in the hand, and the result is shown in the photograph (*left*). A less formal bunch of randomly arranged, scented herbs and flowers is known as a tussie-mussie, and originated in the Middle Ages. At that time, it was very fashionable to carry a tussie-mussie, because the fragrance of the flowers (which included sweet peas) was believed to ward off contagious diseases such as the plague. A tussie-mussie certainly provided respite from the stench of the times, but was unlikely to guard against jail fever (which we call typhoid), despite being carried by the recorders of the law courts.

Above: Sweet peas look best with other light and fluffy flowers, as in this Victorian posy. I chose peach and cream sweet peas, then added concentric rings of *Haemanthus* for its blood-red feathery flowers, *Asclepias* 'Cinderella' to match the 'Black Tea' roses (*Rosa*), and love-in-the-mist (*Nigella damascena*) seed heads. An outer ruff of *Galax* leaves completes the posy, which was tied with raffia. Posies like this are ideal for summer weddings, especially as sweet peas do not like being wired. They are very effective flowers for decorating pew ends in churches because they last for several hours without water.

Right: Sweet peas are perfect for posies and are mixed here with the textured spires of *Limonium suworowii*,

Japanese anemones (*Anemone japonica*), loosestrife (*Lysimachia*) and toad lilies (*Tricyrtis formosana*).

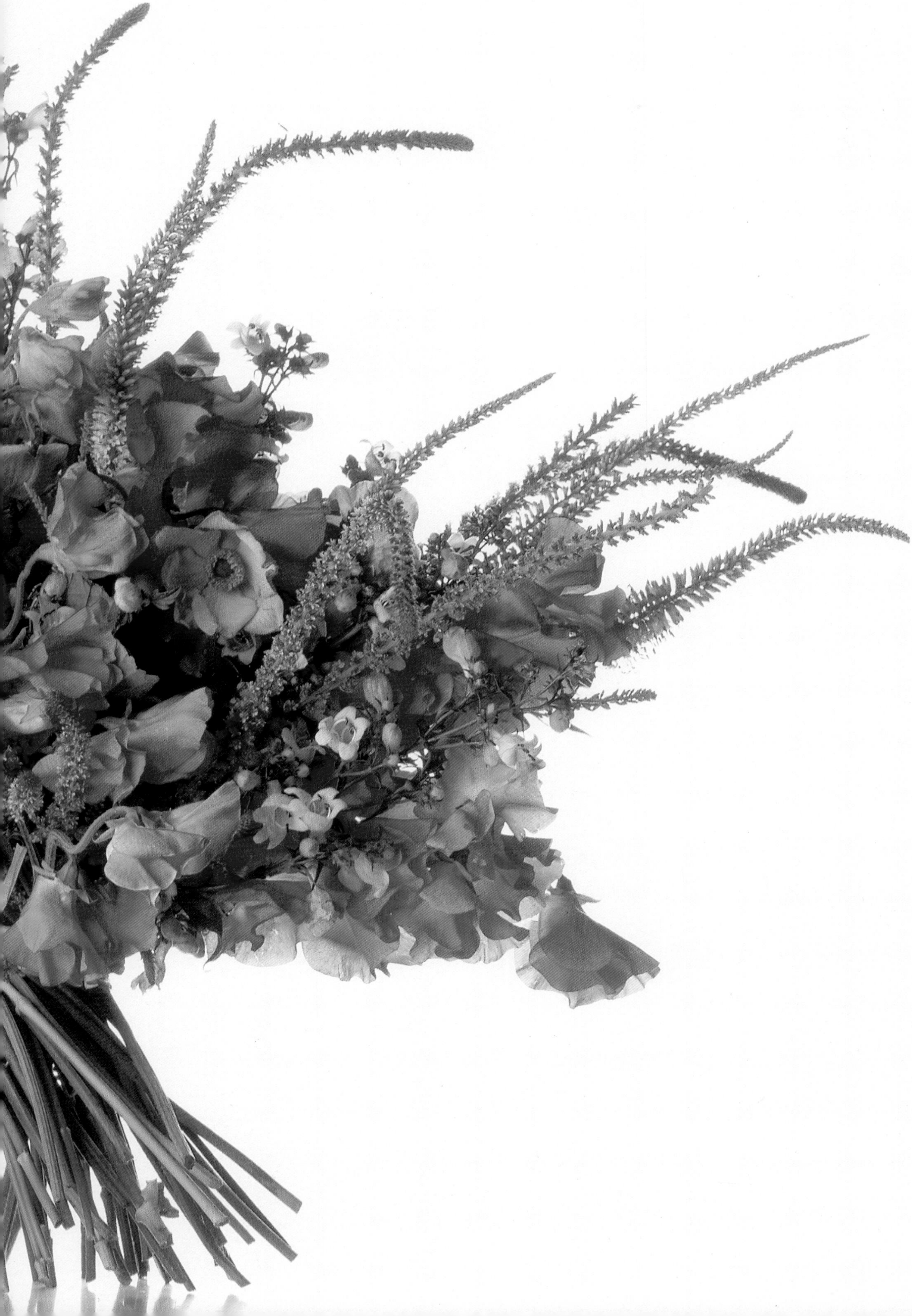

Above, from left to right: Different varieties of *Leucospermum cordifolium*, which are also known as nutans or pin cushions, have subtle variations in shading and colour: *L. c.* 'Red Sunset'; *L. c.* 'Flamespike'; *P.* x 'Carnival'; *P. repens* 'White Repens'; *L. c.* 'Scarlet Ribbon'.

Right: Proteas are the national flower of South Africa and it is here that most species can be found. The head of the family is without doubt the king protea (*Protea cynaroides*), shown here. These statuesque, furry, pink flowers last tremendously well and always look impressive. They are available all year around, although they are at their peak from September to May.

P R O T E A S

This gigantic family of over 60 genera and 1400 species deserves a book to itself rather than a chapter. Originally from Australia and Africa, these exotic, unusual flowers are now widely cultivated in hot, arid climates the world over, including Israel and the Americas. There are four family members which are easily available and suitable for flower arranging – proteas (*Protea*) themselves, banksia (*Banksia*), leucospermum (*Leucospermum*) and leucadendron (*Leucadendron*). Within these species there are hundreds of different varieties that appear on the market at particular times of the year, and all add colour, texture and an architectural quality to floral arrangements.

Left: This posy-style vase arrangement mixes green *Leucadendron discolor* 'Green Discolor' with *Berzelia galpinii* 'Baubles', *Leucospermum cordifolium* 'Sunrise', *Lsp. cuneiforme*, arum lilies (*Zantedeschia*), cock's comb (*Celosia*) and *Dianthus* 'Ceram'.

Until recently, I had only seen proteas as single cut flowers which were packaged in boxes, so it came as a great surprise to me when I saw them growing with many flowerheads on one stem. It is possible to order specific varieties of the Proteaceae family for flower arrangements but, since they are shipped in big boxes, the high cost and large quantity means that this is only really worthwhile if you are doing large-scale decoration work. Unless proteas are indigenous to your country, an order takes about ten days to arrive.

To condition proteas, cut off at least 1 inch (2.5 cm) from the base of the woody stems with a sharp pair of secateurs, then strip off the foliage, otherwise it will go black. Leaf-blackening is a particular problem for *P. repens*, *P. compacta*, *P. neriifolia* and *P. magnifica*. Always use bleach to clean the buckets or containers you will be using to remove any bacteria which would otherwise shorten the life of your flowers – this rule applies to all flowers and not just to proteas. Proteas can discolour the water they are in, so be sure to change it frequently. They generate considerable heat so a low temperature and good air circulation are essential otherwise they

Right: Proteas are such large, heavy-stemmed flowers that they need a very sturdy container. Beach pebbles, coloured glass and gum spiders create a rocky, textured base within the glass vase. The arrangement uses *Protea cynaroides*, *P. magnifica* 'Barbigera', *P. neriifolia* and small ornamental pineapples. The twisted twigs are kiwi vines.

will turn mouldy. The best time to purchase a protea is just before the bracts open but when the flower is already perfectly formed. Proteas are excellent for drying and will dry out if left upright, without water, in a vase. Or, they can be air-dried by being hung upside down in a dry, airy environment.

Generally, the pincushion forms of leucospermum are the most widely available varieties of these flowers. Sadly, they do not dry, but they can last as cut flowers for up to three weeks if kept in the correct conditions. All leucospermum varieties must be kept moist after unpacking. *Lsp. cordifolium* grows in many subtle variations and attractive guises.

The banksia is another member of the Proteaceae tribe. The genus was named after John Banks, an Englishman who travelled to Australia with Captain Cook and amassed a large collection of plants. *Banksia serrata* was so-named because of the plant's serrated leaves and subsequent explorers found many more species; to date, more than 70 have been discovered. The plants originally grew in Australia and Tasmania, but they are now chiefly cultivated as a cut flower in South Africa. They have no scent and will last for up to a month. Banksias

Above: An arrangement of *Paphiopedilum* orchids, *Brunia albiflora*, morning glory vine (*Ipomoea hederacea*), *Leucospermum discolor*, pitcher plants (*Sarracemia leucophylla*), red hot pokers (*Kniphofia*), *Leucadendron* 'Sunset', *Dendrobium* 'Maggie Oei', *Lsp. cordifolium*, *Hypericum* and African *Areca*.
Left: *Alpinia purpurata*, *Banksia collina*, *Leucospermum cordifolium* 'Red Sunset', *Protea cynaroides*, *P. grandiceps* and *Waratah*.

can be dried in the same way as proteas, and although they lose a little colour they remain in much the same physical state as when fresh. The bottle-brush effects make these banksias look like giant old-fashioned microphones and the serrated silver leaves contrast with the orange or yellow flowerheads. Often the plants are dyed the most violent colours of pink and blue, which I think looks ridiculous. *B. coccinea* has gray and orange stripes and is the brightest natural variety.

Large proteas look good arranged on their own with a little exotic foliage, such as *Leucadendron argenteum* 'Silvertree', which I buy all year around to add interest to arrangements. In fact, the leucadendron family provides good foliage for all types of arrangements, not just those containing proteas. *L. salignum* has reddish-brown leaves and common varieties such as 'Safari Sunset' are economical to use all year around. At Christmas they add interest to red arrangements and in my shop we use them with red roses for Valentine's Day. Some of the less common varieties are good for winter decorations because they look like cones and provide extra foliage at a time when it can be in short supply.

WREATH OF PROTEAS

MATERIALS

Floral foam ring

Knife

Cordata foliage

King proteas (*Protea cynaroides*)

P. neriifolia

Alpinia speciosa

Mixed bunch of 'Safari Sunset' foliage

Mixed African *Areca* and protea foliage

Leucadendron linifolium

Ornamental pineapples

  (*Ananas bracteatus*)

Mikado reeds

Curly dried reeds

Bun moss

1 Soak the floral foam ring in water. Trim the edges of the ring to create a rounded surface. Cut the *Cordata* leaves into small sprigs and place in the floral foam ring at a steep angle in three groupings. Any small fleshy leaf could be substituted for the *Cordata* foliage if you cannot buy it.

2 Place one king protea in the middle of one grouping, three proteas for the other grouping and choose a different selection of flowers for your third grouping. For this ring, I have used the *Alpinia speciosa* and some 'Safari Sunset' foliage. You can often buy this in small mixed bunches and it is the most economical way to experiment with South African flowers.

3 Continue adding the flowers around the original groupings, choosing different textures and colours so they contrast with one another. I have used

groups of three or five of each flower because this works well visually, but use your eye to guide you – you do not have to follow any formal rules. Arrange the group of swirly dried reeds through the flowers and foliage to give movement. When you are happy with your groups, pin clumps of bun moss over the floral foam between the groupings. Bun moss provides a good green contrast to the muted tones of the proteas, and 'Safari Sunset' foliage is an inexpensive way to fill an arrangement.

Cover the other two gaps in the foam with bun moss, then add the pineapples and more groups of foliage and reeds (*right*). Check that no floral foam is showing, then spray the ring heavily with a mister. The ring can be soaked in water at a later date in order to prolong the life of the arrangement.

INDEX OF LATIN NAMES

GENERAL INDEX

ACKNOWLEDGMENTS

This book has been pleasure to put together because I have worked with so many very talented and professional people. It is a joint project between myself and Kevin Summers, who is an extremely accomplished photographer. I am really grateful to him for working on this book with me and for being so generous with his time and his expertise. Kevin's resourceful assistants Cameron Watt, Lesley Davies, Derek Kinsella and Colin Campbell have all been very supportive too.

The idea of Kevin and I working together first came from Jacqui Small. She has amazing foresight and we are both grateful to her for enabling us to do a book like this, which began with a joint passion for flowers rather than a project devised in an office. We are also immensely appreciative of Trinity Fry's hard work. Trin spent a great many hours trying to fit all these wonderful images into a book while still finding room for my text. Her dedication has been well beyond the call of normal duty and her skill has to be applauded. Thanks also to Judith More for being understanding, and thanks must also go to my editor, Jane Struthers, who somehow managed to make the writing effortless and great fun.

Thank you to all the hard-working staff at my shop, and particularly to Ashleigh Hopkins for her dedication in running the business. Ashleigh is an extremely gifted designer. Thanks also to Liz Whickendon and Leanne Zenonos, who have been my assistants in the studio and who helped on some of the designs. My grateful appreciation to Gina Jay and my thanks also to the rest of the team at Paula Pryke Flowers: Karen Agnew, John Barry, Emma Brown, Paulette Clarke, Anita Everard, Lizzy Ford, Michelle Geary, Sophie Hindley, Chris Jones, Amanda Lovegrove, Jean Moore, Darren Moss, Ann Pochetty, Tadhg Ryan and Moira Seedhouse.

I am immensely grateful once again to Dennis Edwards at John Austin & Co. Ltd for all his loyal support and practical advice in supplying the wonderful flowers in this book. I have tremendous respect for his knowledge of the flower business and am extremely grateful for his help in supplying and naming these flowers, which often involved making telephone calls to suppliers from all around the world. Thanks also to David, Lee, Chris, Ron, Frank, Perry, Jackie and Tom, my porter.

Many thanks to all the traders at Covent Garden, especially those who have helped with this book: S.R. Allen; John Gardner at Arnott and Mason; David Bacon; Cocquerells; Baker Duguid; David Egan; Charlie Gardiner; Hugh Bradnum and Jeffrey Sparks at Geest; all at Moss; Ted Lawrence at Page Monro; all at Porters; Quality Plants; Martin Brookman at John Ray; Eric Mount at Warmerdam; Barbara Martin at Magnolia Variations; and Something Special. A big thank you to Rinus at Rensen Bloemenexport in Holland for identifying some of the newer flower varieties; Marcel at MHG Flowers; Kees at C. Ros; and Sandro and Silvana Cefolina at Ciesse Flowers in Italy. My grateful thanks also to John Buttery.

Many thanks to Sir Terence Conran and Bridget Bodoano at The Conran Shop; Dean Gipson at Dean Antiques; Kate, Veronica, Nadia and Gilly at the Flowers and Plants Association, whose advice and support have been invaluable; and The Flower Council of Holland. Thanks to Joy Eve, who brought me some wonderful flowers from her country garden. And not forgetting Al Green – don't look back.

Finally, I send my love and gratitude to my extremely supportive family, and to my husband, Peter, who has encouraged in me a love of white spaces.